MAYBERRY TRIVIA

BY SCOTT HOPKINS

LHP

Want to read more about

Andy Griffith and Mayberry?

BEYOND
MAYBERRY

A MEMOIR OF
ANDY GRIFFITH AND
MOUNT AIRY NORTH CAROLINA

THOMAS D. PERRY

Visit Tom Perry's Laurel Hill Publishing

www.freestateofpatrick.com

MAYBERRY TRIVIA

1,500 Questions About A TV Classic

BY SCOTT HOPKINS

LHP

Published by Tom Perry's Laurel Hill Publishing LLC

4443 Ararat Highway

P. O. Box 11

Ararat, VA 24053

www.freestateofpatrick.com

freestateofpatrick@yahoo.com

276-692-5300

Laurel Hill Publishing

www.freestateofpatrick.com

Thomas D. "Tom" Perry
4443 Ararat Highway
P O Box 11
Ararat VA 24053

276-692-5300
freestateofpatrick@yahoo.com
www.freestateofpatrick.com

ISBN/SKU:9780692745762

ISBN Complete:978-0-692-74576-2

Publication Date:7/1/2016

Street Date:7/4/2016

Table of Contents

Make a game out if it !

Correct answers for: True/ False =   1 point
                       Multiple Choice =   2 points
                       General Questions =   3 points

Acknowledgements

I would like to thank the following persons for their help in giving birth to this book: Thomas Perry, Allan Newsome, David Browning, Marcus Kimbrough, Denny McCaughan, Paul Mulik, Jim Clark, Jeff Koontz, Peggy Gray, and Haley Hopkins.

GENERAL QUESTIONS

1) Who travels all the way to Mayberry to shake Barney's hand?

2) What names does the state investigator give to the "three cow thieves"?

3) What is the last name of the state investigator who helps with the cow thief mystery?

4) What is adventure sleeping?

5) How did Barney learn to crochet?

6) What talent does Howard Sprague display on Colonel "Tim's Talent Time?"

7) Name one thing Frank Myers plans to buy after cashing in his bond.

8) According to Andy, who will just "nasty away" when he dies?

9) Where does Mayor Stoner purchase a bed jacket?

10) With whom does Sally like to dance with at O'Malley's cabin?

1) The Governor of North Carolina

2) Able, Baker, and Charlie

3) Upchurch

4) Sleeping on an ironing board between two chairs

5) By watching his mother

6) Comedy (told jokes)

7) Air conditioner/ stove/ color TV/ stereo phonograph

8) Ben Weaver (the old one)

9) Luken's Style Shop

10) Al

11) Who presides over the All Souls Church?

12) Name the state investigator that likes to go frog-gigging with Andy.

13) What is the hometown of the one-man band that traveled through Mayberry?

14) Roy Swanson, Goober's old friend from mechanics school, claims to be a Senior Vice President of what company?

15) What adult education class do Andy, Helen, Goober, and Howard take together?

16) What household product is Aunt Bee's marmalade said to smell like?

17) What is the first name of Charlene Darling's daughter?

18) Who secretly ran a still at the Remshaw house?

19) Andy's business cards are printed with what color of ink?

20) What is the stage name of Irene Phlogg, the movie star from Mayberry?

11) Reverend Hobart M. Tucker

12) Sam Allen

13) Altoona

14) Amalgamated Motors

15) American History

16) Ammonia

17) Andelina

18) Big Jack Anderson

19) Green (same ink used for counterfeit money)

20) Teena Andrews

21) What is a number two amber alert?

22) What comic strip does Barney like to read in the Sunday paper?

23) On what street in Mayberry does the Taylor family live?

24) What gossip column does Red Akin write for the Mayberry Gazette?

25) What item does Aunt Bee ask Bert Miller to sell her?

26) What is the name of the preacher who is to marry Andy and Charlene should her divorce go through?

27) What is the name of the firstborn son of farmer Sam Becker?

28) Name one karate move Barney demonstrates for Andy.

29) Whose phone number is 426?

30) What does Nelvin display to keep people off his property?

31) Which world summit is held in Mayberry?

32) What escaped criminal says, "I'm gonna get you for this, deputy?"

33) What two people were arrested August 9, 1946, for the "punch in the nose" incident?

34) How was the first "punch in the nose" incident settled?

21) Either Andy or Barney awake at all times

22) Andy Gump

23) Maple Street, Elm Street, or Maple Road

24) Mayberry after Midnight

25) An apron

26) Preacher Winslow

27) Andy

28) The hawk, the bull elk, or the rattlesnake.

29) Andy's

30) Quarantine signs

31) US/USSR summit

32) Eddie Brook

33) Charlie Foley and Floyd Lawson

34) With a forgiving handshake and a free shave

35) Who does Mrs. Wiley think is from Back Bay Boston?

36) Who writes down the steps to take while on a date?

37) Where is Ronald Bailey headed when he has a traffic accident?

38) With whom does Floyd correspond in a lonely hearts club?

39) Name one of the Mayberry jewelry stores.

40) What substance do Opie and Tray Bowden use to seal their bond as blood brothers?

41) What couple met at Wilton Blair's funeral in 1960?

42) What does Barney say Andy's reelection campaign slogan should be?

43) What book does Andy suggest Barney should write on how to "probe the subconscious mind"?

44) What is Barney's address?

45) What does Barney say is his number one job?

46) Who is the author of "Poems of Romance"?

47) Why was Effie Bartlett in the back room of Monroe's Funeral Parlor and TV Repair?

35) Ernest T. Bass posing as Oliver Gossage

36) Goober

37) Miami

38) Madeline Grayson

39) Barclay's Jewelry or Sterling's Jewelry

40) Barn paint

41) Barney and Thelma Lou

42) "Win with Taylor"

43) Barney Fife Subconscious Prober Primer

44) 411 Elm Street

45) Stalking (not fly killing)

46) T. Jonathon Osgood

47) Her picture tube went out.

48) What is Barney's nickname for Mrs. Lesch?

49) How does Barney describe Halcyon Loretta Winslow's physical appearance?

50) What is the name of Aunt Bee's cooking show?

51) Who is said to be the town jinx?

52) What does Frank Myers do for a living?

53) Who does Ben Weaver say is the best salesman in Mayberry?

54) What treatment does Barney want to give the state inspector who is helping with the cow thief mystery?

55) Who really owns the "stray" dogs in the episode "Dogs, Dogs, Dogs?"

56) Who is the masked singer?

57) Who is Ben Weaver's night watchman?

58) In addition to County Clerk, what other job does Howard Sprague hold in Mayberry?

59) Where do Opie and his friends play Robin Hood?

60) In what city does Andy meet with a female attorney?

61) In what year was The Feed and Grain store established?

62) Who is Thelma Lou's homely cousin?

48) Hubcaps Lesch

49) Beasto Moristo, Ugliest girl you ever saw in your life

50) The Mayberry Chef

51) Henry Bennett

52) Makes berries for women's hats

53) Andy

54) The big freeze

55) Clint Biggers

56) Leonard Blush

57) Asa Breeney

58) News reporter (the garden column), Floyd's landlord

59) Crouch's Woods

60) Raleigh

61) 1890

62) Mary Grace Gossage

63) What state inmates sent a Christmas card to Andy and Barney?

64) Who is Barney's judo instructor?

65) Who is the big shot-publisher who gets a speeding ticket from Andy?

66) What type of letter does Barney want to use to scare the Miracle Salve Company?

67) Who accidentally sets fire to Jubal Foster's barn?

68) What does Mrs. Lesch say was the name of her late husband?

69) Who is The Man in a Hurry?

70) Who is Floyd's nephew?

71) What brand of vacuum cleaner did Barney once peddle?

72) Who, along with his female partner, robs the furniture company payroll?

73) What is the name of the Mayberry ice cream parlor?

74) What is the name of the gentleman who records folk music featuring various Mayberrians?

75) What is the name of the legendary silver carp in Tucker's Lake?

76) What is Leon's favorite sandwich?

63) The Hubacher Brothers

64) Mr. Izamoto

65) J. Howard Jackson

66) A lawyer letter

67) Jubal Foster

68) Bernard Lesch

69) Malcolm Tucker

70) Warren Ferguson

71) Miracle Sweep

72) "Doc" Clarence Malloy

73) Murphy's House of the Nine Flavors

74) Mr. Maxwell

75) Old Sam

76) Peanut butter and jelly

77) What illegal crop does Barney think Sam Becker is planting?

78) What farmer comes to town to find a wife?

79) Who loses a purse with $50 in it?

80) Who is the stranger that adopts Mayberry as his hometown?

81) How many guitars does Jim Lindsey own after he becomes "famous?"

82) Name Barney's speed trap set up on Highway 6.

83) What bird supposedly leads Barney and Gomer back to camp?

84) Who is the traveling handyman who stays with the Taylors?

85) According to Opie, who is the prettiest girl in the first grade?

86) Who is the "spoiled kid" who rides his bike on the sidewalks?

87) Name Mayberry's most popular band.

88) Who is the pancake-eating champion of Mayberry?

77) Marijuana

78) Jeff Pruitt

79) Parnell Rigsby

80) Ed Sawyer

81) Three

82) Checkpoint Chickie

83) Web-footed, Red-crested Lake Loon

84) Henry Wheeler

85) Mary Wiggins

86) Arnold Winkler

87) Bobby Fleet (or Freddie Fleet) and his Band with a Beat.

88) Goober

89) Goober says he doesn't know much, but he does know about what two things?

90) What happens when Lydia Croswaith goes out in the sun?

91) Who punches Otis in the nose for siding with Floyd in the nose-punching incident of 1946?

92) How much money does Barney estimate the Mayberry Bank contains on a typical Friday night?

93) Name any three of Andy's girlfriends.

94) What local businessman does Aunt Bee almost marry?

95) How does Barney know when Andy is mad?

96) As a youth, on what animal did Floyd practice his barbering skills?

97) What does Mary Pleasant hunt while vacationing in the Great Dismal Swap?

98) Who is a notary public in Mayberry?

99) What is Andy's favorite dish?

100) Should Helen ever marry, what would she regularly prepare for her husband's meals?

89) Cars and guns

90) She gets the herpes

91) Lamar Tuttle

92) $50,000

93) Ellie, Peggy, Helen, Mary, Sharon, Alice, or Barbara Edwards

94) Mr. Goss

95) His jaw muscles start working

96) Alley cats

97) Black bears

98) Mary Pleasant

99) Leg of lamb

100) Frozen dinners

101) How does Sally, the escaped convict, remember "Al" liking his hamburgers?

102) How old was Goober when Mr. Foley punched Floyd in the nose in 1946?

103) Who was the first sheriff who settled Mr. Foley's and Floyd Lawson's assault incident?

104) What does Opie want to win for his dad at the shooting gallery?

105) To what major city did Andy's high school sweetheart move after they broke up?

106) Who was Andy's high school sweetheart?

107) What are Otis' normal nights to stay at the Mayberry jail?

108) To what city had Charlie O'Malley gone shortly before the female convicts stayed at his cabin?

109) How does Aunt Bee describe the condition of Andy's bedroom to Thelma Lou?

110) On what day of the week does the Mayberry "knot tying club" meet?

111) What type of animal footprint does Opie make in the ground that sends Barney into a panic?

112) What wild animal does Barney think is stealing food during a Mayberry dry spell?

101) Hard

102) Five

103) Poindexter

104) Electric Razor

105) Chicago or Philadelphia

106) Sharon DeSpain

107) Friday and Saturday

108) Detroit

109) An elephant's nest

110) Tuesday

111) Elephant

112) Fox

113) How much does Otis pay for a cow that he thinks is a horse?

114) What does Ernest T. Bass want to get from the U. S. military?

115) On what night of the week do Barney and Thelma Lou regularly watch TV and eat cashew fudge?

116) Who tells Opie that horsehair can be turned into a snake?

117) Who tells Opie that chewing tar is good for the teeth?

118) In which cell does Otis prefer to sleep?

119) What is Otis' day job?

120) Who did Opie once handcuff to the school flagpole?

121) Who wins an award as Mayberry's most distinguished citizen?

122) What does Barney keep under his hat?

123) Where does Barney move when he leaves Mayberry?

124) How much money does Opie donate to The Underprivileged Children's Fund?

125) What is the nickname Otis gives to "warden" Aunt Bee?

126) How much money does Opie need for milk money?

127) What is the name of Luke Jenson's dog?

113) $20

114) A uniform

115) Tuesday

116) Johnny Paul Jason

117) Johnny Paul Jason

118) Number one (on the right)

119) Glue dipper at the furniture factory

120) Ralph Baker

121) Otis

122) Citation pad or money

123) Raleigh

124) Three cents

125) Bloody Mary

126) Five cents

127) Mack

128) How many blue ribbons does Clara win for her pickles?

129) What town offers Barney the position of sheriff?

130) What instrument does Barney play in the town band?

131) What key does Bobby Fleet say that Jim Lindsey finds while tuning his guitar?

132) What was the name of Gomer's dog?

133) For how much money does Otis sue the county for gross negligence?

134) Who is Otis' lawyer?

135) What is the name of Otis' imaginary dog?

136) What did Barney give his parents for their wedding anniversary?

137) Who does Barney say is standing "naked" before him during a psychological exam?

138) What does Otis see during the inkblot test?

139) With whom does Barney frequently sip cider on the front porch?

140) Who does Aunt Bee say should win the Mayberry beauty contest?

141) How many pairs of shoes does Mr. Wilbur Finch sell in Mayberry?

128) Twelve (that we know of)

129) Greendale

130) Cymbals

131) Key of "S"

132) Sport

133) $5,000

134) Neil Bentley

135) Spot

136) A septic tank

137) Otis

138) A Bat

139) Mrs. Mendelbright

140) Ellie Walker

141) 67 pairs

142) How does Otis describe the act of Barney and Andy taking him home to his wife rather than letting him stay in the jail cell?

143) What is the name of Otis' wife?

144) What is the highest dollar offer Mayor Stoner makes for Andy's fishing pole?

145) Other than Sunday, on what day is the Mayberry Gazette published?

146) What instrument does Barney play to entertain Mary, Andy, and Thelma Lou?

147) What animal is named Jimmy?

148) What is the name of Aunt Bee's Chinese restaurant?

149) What brand of gas does Wally's service station sell?

150) What is the retail price of a jar of miracle salve?

151) Where is the extra key to Walker's drug store kept?

152) Where does Andy keep his handgun at home?

153) Who told Opie that a penny struck by lightning is worth six cents?

154) To what city is Malcolm Tucker headed when his car breaks down, stranding him in Mayberry?

155) In "The Pickle Story," how many quarts of pickles did Aunt Bee make in total?

142) Police brutality

143) Rita

144) $27.50

145) Wednesday

146) Bongo drums

147) Goat

148) Aunt Bee's Canton Palace

149) Acme

150) 35 cents

151) Above the front door

152) On top of the hutch/cabinet

153) Nat Pike

154) Charlotte

155) 24

156) Who cannot put up shingles on the Taylor's roof because of a bad back?

157) What is Opie playing with when he kills a songbird?

158) Why is Gomer reluctant to crawl under the bandstand?

159) Where are the spare keys to the squad car kept?

160) Who was the only cast member to portray the same Mayberry role for ten consecutive years?

161) Where was The Andy Griffith Show filmed?

162) On what TV show was the character Sheriff Andy Taylor introduced?

163) What year was the final regular season for The Andy Griffith Show?

164) How many Emmy Awards did Don Knotts win for his portrayal of Barney Fife?

165) What is the name of Cousin Gloria's fiancé?

166) Who tries to swindle Mrs. Mendelbright?

167) How many documented cases of malfeasance does Barney have against the Mayberry sheriff's department?

168) Whom did actor Bill Bixby portray on The Andy Griffith Show?

169) What is the name of Clara Edwards' son?

156) Henry Wheeler

157) A slingshot

158) He's afraid of spiders

159) Top drawer of the courthouse desk

160) Francis Bavier as Aunt Bee

161) Desilu Studios in Hollywood, 40 Acres backlot, Culver City

162) The Danny Thomas Show

163) 1968

164) Five

165) Frank

166) Oscar Fields

167) 76

168) Ron Bailey

169) Gale

170) Name an abnormal sound Gilly Walker's car makes.

171) How many hatfuls of water does Briscoe Darling say his truck's radiator holds?

172) How many children do Uncle Ollie and Aunt Nora have?

173) What excuse does Uncle Ollie give for cutting short his family's trip to Mayberry?

174) How many pounds of beef does Aunt Bee purchase from "Diamond Jim's?"

175) With whom does Clara Edwards "keep steady company?"

176) What is the first name of the gentleman who is to repair Helen's television set?

177) Why does Andy say he holds in his stomach when Charlene Darling is around?

178) What public utility does Newton Monroe hit while digging behind the courthouse?

179) What is the name of Mayberry's coffee shop?

180) What movie star's house do the Taylors see while in Hollywood?

181) What is wrong with Malcolm Tucker's car?

182) How far outside of town does Malcolm Tucker's car break down?

183) Who is cast in the role of Sheriff Taylor in the movie "Sheriff without a Gun?"

170) Pucka pucka pucka, pa-ding pa-ding, or chah-wee, chah-wee

171) Eleven

172) Two

173) He left the gas stove and the radio on

174) 150

175) Clark Cooper

176) George (played by Howard Morris)

177) She makes him nervous

178) A water pipe

179) Dave's or Klein's

180) Cesar Romero's

181) Clogged fuel line

182) Two miles

183) Bryan Bender (played by Gavin McLeod)

184) What resident of Mayberry claims to have ESP?

185) What woman fills in for Goober at Wally's while he is on vacation?

186) What is described by Gomer as "a picture no artist could draw?"

187) What is the minimum weight requirement set forth by the state in order to be a deputy sheriff?

188) What foreign language did Floyd study in barber college?

189) Who is the gentleman who says, "Tomorrow: the perfect day to start any job?"

190) Who is to be evicted from his house so that a new highway can be built?

191) Whom is Andy forced to evict for back unpaid taxes?

192) What is George Foley's hometown?

193) How much money does Barney want to donate to Mr. Lesch's favorite charity?

194) Whom does Ernest T. Bass hit in the head with a rock while courting her?

195) In high school, Aunt Bee had a "real bent" toward which subject?

196) Who, according to Barney, is the biggest gossip in town?

184) Warren

185) Flora

186) Mr. Johnson's farm

187) 145 pounds

188) Latin

189) Dave Browne

190) Mr. Frisby

191) Frank Myers

192) Eastmont

193) $2.50

194) Hogette Winslow

195) Chemistry

196) Viola Slatt

197) According to Annabelle Silby, how did her husband die?

198) Among what Indian tribe does Colonel Harvey claim to have lived?

199) According to Floyd, where do you have to go to get a good suit?

200) Where did Helen Crump live prior to Mayberry?

201) In which direction does Barney ride a horse to make Charlene Darling's divorce null and void?

202) From what store did Barney buy the shirt he was to wear while squiring the Apricot Queen?

203) What number does Henry Bennett need to draw from the hat to win a portable TV?

204) What number does Henry Bennett pull out of the hat at the church raffle?

205) For whom did Opie save his money in order to buy a coat?

206) When Barney commands, "All right three, step out!" who steps out?

207) According to the new state requirements, how tall does Barney need to be in order to be a deputy sheriff?

208) What item does Ernest T. Bass break over a man's head at Mrs. Wiley's party?

209) According to a magazine ad, who is growing mushrooms in the basement for fun and profit?

197) Hit by a taxi

198) Shawnee

199) Mt. Pilot

200) Kansas City, Kansas

201) East to West

202) Patterson's

203) Forty Four

204) 6 7/8

205) Charlotte

206) Goober and Otis

207) 5' 8"

208) A vase

209) 209. V. J. of Cincinnati

210) According to Johnny Paul, how long do you have to live if you lick the point of an indelible pencil?

211) How much does Andy want Opie to donate to The Underprivileged Children's Fund?

212) Whose initials are scratched on the town cannon?

213) How long does Barney spend polishing his hat for the Chamber of Commerce dance?

214) What is Gomer studying to be?

215) How much does it cost Ernest T. Bass to get a "gold tooth?"

216) What does Andy tell Madeline Grayson his middle name is?

217) What does Andy tell Madeline Grayson he is studying to be?

218) What dessert does Andy like after a businessman's special lunch?

219) What famous actor appeared on TAGS as a man whose distraught wife left their baby on the courthouse steps?

220) What type of candy bar does Barney pack for lunch?

221) What building does Barney enjoy watching while they change the marquee?

222) While pretending to be a big spender, how much does Barney say he paid for his cigars?

223) While pretending to be a big spender, how many cigars does Barney say he plans to smoke per day?

210) One and one half minutes

211) At least 50 cents or one dollar

212) Tracy Rupert

213) Three hours

214) A Doctor

215) One dollar

216) Paul

217) A Chiropractor

218) A yellow cookie

219) Jack Nicholson

220) Mr. Cookie bar

221) The Grand

222) "35 cents a copy"

223) Eight

224) What waitress is a widow with four children?

225) What is the front part of the alphabet, according to Ernest T. Bass?

226) What did Aunt Bee call the meal she served Colonel Harvey?

227) Who climbs a tree every time he has a fight with his wife?

228) Where does Warren Ferguson hail from?

229) Who locks herself in a cell to escape from Warren's romantic advances?

230) Whom is Bobby Gribble engaged to marry?

231) What item does Aunt Bee lose, prompting Andy to file an insurance claim?

232) What is the name of Andy's insurance agent?

233) What does Aunt Bee buy with her insurance money?

234) What talisman does Opie give to Mr. Tucker?

235) For how many re-runs of The Andy Griffith Show did Don Knotts' contract include royalties?

236) Who offers Andy and Barney some hog backbone for dinner?

237) Who is the Mayberry Postmaster?

238) Who eats most of the apricots in Mayberry?

239) Who is the Arkansas women's skeet shooting champion?

224) Olive

225) ABCFLG

226) Pot luck

227) Mr. Pervis

228) Boston

229) Helen

230) Emma Lars

231) A pin

232) Ed Jenkins

233) A garbage disposal

234) A penny run over by a train

235) Four

236) Charlene Darling

237) Billy Ray Talbot

238) Barney

239) Karen Moore

240) What is a code 710?

241) What is the name of the trailer park where Malloy and his female partner hide out?

242) What town is television station WZAZ located in?

243) When is the Leonard Blush show broadcast?

244) What vegetable twangs Briscoe Darling's buds?

245) While out camping, what type of bird does Barney claim to have ensnared?

246) What two Mt. Pilot radio stations broadcast the Leonard Blush show?

247) According to Gomer, why does Merle Dean's truck squeak when he bounces on the fender?

248) Who is known as a "tiller of soil and feller of trees"?

249) For Barney's sake, why does Andy cancel the subscription to the Police Gazette?

250) What cat has Andy been friends with for years?

251) How many rules are there at "the rock?"

252) How much money did Andy and Barney get for their old Model A after it gave out on their trip to New Orleans?

240) Assault with a deadly weapon

241) Half moon trailer park

242) Raleigh

243) Third Tuesday of each month

244) Pearly onions

245) Wild Pheasant

246) YLRB and WMPT

247) Bad Shocks

248) Briscoe Darling

249) It contained girlie pictures

250) Fluffy

251) Two

252) $12.00

253) Whose campaign poster looks like he is sniffing out crime?

254) What is the name of the Mayberry little league baseball team?

255) How long does it take for Fred Goss' special service when you are in a rush?

256) While Gomer is perched on the courthouse roof, whom does he witness taking a dip of snuff?

257) What city does Barney refer to as another Dodge City?

258) From which city does John Masters order a choral arrangement of "Santa Lucia?"

259) For what traffic violation does Andy stop Danny Williams (Danny Thomas)?

260) For what holiday does Andy consider a beer can opener with an umbrella on it to be a nice gift?

261) Where are 946 jars of Miracle Salve delivered?

262) What man, on occasion, answers the phone at the diner, embarrassing Barney?

263) What is the name of Andy's boat?

253) Barney's

254) The Giants

255) 255. Three hours

256) Viola McConker

257) Greendale

258) New York

259) Running a stop sign

260) Mother's Day

261) The Taylor house (to Opie Taylor, Sr.)

262) Frank

263) Gertrude

264) What was the original cost of Frank Myers' bond?

265) Who sells an organ to the All Souls Church?

266) Clarence Earp is told that his last name is not actually Earp, but what?

267) When Ernest T. crashes Mrs. Wiley's party, he sticks his hand in the punchbowl and eats every bit of what?

268) What is Barney's shoe size?

269) What is Halcyon Loretta Winslow's occupation?

270) According to Barney, who is a "blonde from a bottle"?

271) What is the fine for making an illegal U-turn in Mayberry?

272) How long did Henry Gilley court Tyla Lee Vernon before they got married?

273) Where does Myra Koonce work?

274) How much money is Barney looking to blow at Hialeah Race Track?

275) Who is a licensed PPD?

276) In what city does Jim Lindsey buy a guitar pick?

277) Where does Oscar Skinner work?

264) $100 (Confederate)

265) Mr. Hendricks

266) Dempsey

267) The watermelon rind

268) 7 ½ B

269) Prune pitter

270) Sue Grigsby

271) Five dollars

272) 16 years

273) The lingerie shop

274) $200

275) Dr. Merle Osmond

276) Winston-Salem

277) The Feed and Grain store

278) How much does Barney charge the sheriff's office for replacing the pea in his whistle?

279) What boy is planning on running away to Texas?

280) What does Orville Hendricks sell?

281) What word did Goober pick up in the National Guard?

282) Who leaves the lid of the soup can in Barney's soup?

283) Which cast member is from Jasper, Alabama?

284) According to Goober, how many hours is a long time to go without eating?

285) What is the posted speed limit on Highway 6?

286) How much money is supposedly taken in the Great Walker Drug Store Robbery?

287) What does Clarabelle Morrison like the smell of?

288) Who always carries an extra shoelace with him?

289) Who owns a Teddy Roosevelt horse pistol?

290) Who makes a tree out of newspaper for Opie?

291) As a youth, who won a medal in the 50-yard dash?

292) How many times was Barney's column in the school newspaper published?

278) Nothing

279) George Foley

280) Butter and Eggs

281) Yo

282) Malcolm Merriweather

283) George Lindsey (Goober)

284) Three

285) 35 mph

286) 24 dollars

287) Witch Hazel Lotion

288) Gomer

289) Asa Breeney

290) Malcolm Merriweather

291) Barney

292) One

293) What composer "sorta does it" for Thelma Lou?

294) To which building does Barney give a police escort to Melissa Stevens, the new girl in town?

295) What does Effie Bartlett like to watch on TV?

296) Whom does Otis hit with a leg of lamb?

297) Floyd wants a statue erected in honor of what former Mayberrian?

298) After Goober buys the gas station, how many gallons of gas per week does he pump?

299) Who buys a purple tie for his date with Mary Grace Gossage?

300) What does shoe salesman Wilbur Finch purchase at the drug store?

301) Why is the salt and pepper suit special to Barney?

302) What is the name of Opie's imaginary horse?

303) How much does Andy insist Opie should save from the $50 that he finds?

304) Who runs a still at Hawks Point?

305) What does Barney tell Aunt Bee he has in the suitcase when we he is supposedly going to visit his cousin?

293) Cole Porter

294) The Post Office

295) Wrestling

296) His mother-in-law

297) Daniel Lawson

298) Eighty

299) Gomer

300) Root beer

301) It is just right for the dip (while dancing)

302) Blackie

303) $40

304) Ben Sewell

305) Shaving lotion

306) Midnight Madness perfume makes Andy smell like what?

307) What are the school colors of Mayberry Union High?

308) What is Emmett the fix-it man's last name?

309) How many guns normally sit in the courthouse gun rack?

310) Whom does Aunt Bee "beat" with a wooden spoon?

311) Who permanently replaces Barney as Deputy Sheriff?

312) What does Goober purchase from Newton Monroe?

313) Who was the material witness in the Floyd vs. Foley nose-punching case?

314) What does Floyd buy from Newton Monroe?

315) What does Ben Weaver give Opie for Christmas?

316) Facing the courthouse doors, how many windows are in the front of the Mayberry Courthouse?

317) Who is supposedly a great-nephew of Wyatt Earp?

318) The drugstore serves a hollowed out tomato stuffed with what?

319) What mayor does Barney arrest?

306) A gardenia blossom or the beauty parlor

307) Orange and blue

308) Clark

309) Six

310) Briscoe Darling

311) Warren Ferguson

312) A transistor radio

313) Goober

314) A watch

315) Roller skates

316) Two

317) Clarence

318) Avocado and raisins

319) Mayor Pike

320) What is inscribed on the back of Barney's five-year anniversary gift?

321) What Mayberrian is a somnambulist?

322) How many bottles of Colonel Harvey's Indian Elixir does Aunt Bee purchase?

323) What item does Barney's "bloodhound" learn to fetch?

324) Which one of Helen's dresses is Andy partial to?

325) What bachelor is always smiling and talking to himself?

326) Who said maybe Thelma Lou wasn't meant for Barney?

327) Who refers to Helen as a third party?

328) Who calls Helen a dame?

329) Who says the best things in life are free?

330) Who receives credit for capturing the three women convicts?

331) Who receives a fine for sweeping trash into the street?

332) Who calls Gomer a boob?

333) Who breaks the replacement glass for the courthouse before it is installed?

320) "Five" or "5"

321) Warren Ferguson

322) Two

323) The cell keys

324) The green one

325) Jed McEntire

326) Barney

327) Andy

328) Barney

329) Barney

330) Floyd

331) Fred Plummer

332) Barney

333) Barney (he put his gun through it)

334) Which Mayberry law officer issues a ticket to himself?

335) Which code number is violated if you turn in a false alarm?

336) What was Gomer doing just prior to making a U-turn on Main Street?

337) What time does Barney tell his campaign truck driver to cease advertising?

338) What is Otis' specialty while supposedly working for the sheriff's department?

339) Who is the accompanist for the Mayberry town choir?

340) Why didn't Jess Morgan report back to the jail to finish his sentence?

341) What does Ben Weaver give Ellie Walker for Christmas?

342) Who claims to go to church with witches?

343) What restaurant will let you take in a bottle of liquor?

344) What is the matter with Helen Crump's TV set?

334) Barney

335) 785

336) Visiting the post office

337) 9 o'clock PM

338) Tracking down stills

339) Hazel

340) He got treed by a bear

341) Perfume

342) The Darlings

343) Morelli's

344) The linear control is completely shot

345) Who is the "star witness" when Otis falls in the courthouse?

346) Where does Mary Pleasant work?

347) What causes Otis to fall outside the cell and injure his knee?

348) What does Floyd think Neil Bentley's suit is made of?

349) How does Otis say he received his old football injury?

350) Who "blew up" the chemistry class?

351) Who sometimes takes anti-acid tablets?

352) What is Barney in charge of when he moves to Raleigh?

353) Who moves out of town a month after Barney leaves?

354) Barney gave Aunt Bee a handkerchief that was made where?

355) To what city does Thelma Lou move when she leaves Mayberry?

356) Who gets a nosebleed when he is slapped in the face?

357) Name the person Thelma Lou marries after she leaves Mayberry.

345) Floyd

346) The bank

347) He tripped on his own coat

348) Sharkskin

349) Playing football with his wife

350) Albert Kitcherly

351) Barney

352) Fingerprints, section N-R

353) Thelma Lou

354) Tijuana

355) Jacksonville

356) Barney

357) Gerald Whitfield

358) What does Aunt Bee put over her car to hide a damaged fender?

359) Who accidentally drives his car into the back of Aunt Bee's car?

360) According to Goober, at what time do you need to get to the drugstore to get the good slices of corned beef?

361) Prior to having headlights on the truck, what did the Darlings use to see at night?

362) According to Aunt Bee, what is the minimum courtship period in Mayberry?

363) Who falls victim to the Omen of the Owl?

364) What animal sits on the mantle at Andy's lodge?

365) Where does Aunt Nora live?

366) Name two of Aunt Bee's three sisters.

367) How many pairs of socks does Opie take with him on his overnight trip with the Boy Scouts?

368) According to Andy, what is the only excuse for not eating at mealtime?

369) What is the secret ingredient in Goober's spaghetti sauce?

370) How many years has The Andy Griffith Show been off the air since its debut?

358) Opie's tent

359) Andy

360) About 12:30

361) They held a lantern out over the hood.

362) One year

363) Helen Crump

364) A stuffed owl

365) Lake Charles

366) Ellen, Nora, or Florence

367) Five

368) Sickness

369) Oregano

370) Zero

371) What Mayberrian buys Floyd's barbershop?

372) How many years had Floyd operated his barbershop in Mayberry before it was sold?

373) As a child, what did Andy try to eat in Floyd's barbershop?

374) Name the realtor who sells Floyd's Barbershop.

375) Who beats up Harold Lovitt?

376) Who unsuccessfully attempts to cut Opie's hair while Floyd's is temporarily closed?

377) Whom does Mr. McCabe call a "dropout?"

378) What Russian raids the Taylor icebox in the middle of the night?

379) What subject does Andy tell a group of boys was hard for him when he was growing up?

380) What historical events does Andy tell the boys about to get them interested in American history?

381) What is the name of the Mayberry boys' history troop?

382) Who demonstrates smoke signals using his cigar?

383) What type of cake does Aunt Bee not allow in the Taylor house?

371) Howard Sprague

372) 28 years

373) Shaving cream (he thought it was ice cream)

374) Harry Walker

375) The Ferguson girl

376) Aunt Bee

377) Barney

378) Mr. Vasidovich

379) History

380) The shot heard 'round the world / the ride of Paul Revere

381) The Mayberry Minutemen

382) Colonel Harvey

383) Fruitcake

384) What is the name of the state investigator who is to determine if the Mayberry sheriff's office needs extra funds?

385) What type of food does Otis say is bad for his liver?

386) How do you wake Barney out of a sound sleep?

387) What odorous entrée does the diner serve on Tuesdays?

388) What does Barney say he was "born" with in his hand?

389) What does Barney buy Opie after he lets his wild birds go free?

390) According to Barney, what is the biggest cause of goldfish deaths?

391) What TAGS actor went on to appear as the star of the TV show Happy Days?

392) What actor - besides Don Knotts - won an Emmy for working on The Andy Griffith Show?

393) What character from The Andy Griffith Show went on to have his own major TV show?

394) Who is Mayberry's most popular barber?

395) What business sponsors the Mayberry Rollers bowling team?

396) Which state is Mayberry located in?

384) Mr. Somerset

385) Spicy food, Soda pop

386) Snap of the fingers

387) Corned Beef and Cabbage

388) A slingshot

389) A fishbowl and some goldfish

390) Overfeeding

391) Ron Howard

392) Frances Bavier (Aunt Bee)

393) Gomer Pyle

394) Floyd Lawson

395) Emmett's Fix-It Shop

396) North Carolina

397) Who brews moonshine in their greenhouse?

398) What is last name of Andy's cousin in Mayberry?

399) What is the name of Mayberry's main filling station?

400) What name does Barney use when he poses as a veterinarian?

401) Who is the Mayberry town drunk?

402) What is Opie's relationship to Leon in real life?

403) What is the name of Andy Griffith's hometown?

404) What object does Barney toss at Goober in the deputy lineup?

405) Who finds a mousetrap in the Taylor's freezer?

406) What animal does Barney say is selfish?

407) Opie breaks a display bottle of what expensive perfume at the drugstore?

408) Who portrayed a manicurist in one TAGS episode before becoming a famous TV star?

409) What is the last name of the music-playing family from the mountains who occasionally visit Mayberry?

410) Who mistakenly receives straight A's on one report card?

397) The Morrison sisters

398) Fife

399) Wally's Service Station (later, Goober's Service Station)

400) U.T. Pendyke, DVM

401) Otis Campbell

402) They are brothers (Ronny and Clint Howard)

403) Mt. Airy, North Carolina

404) An egg

405) Gomer

406) Giraffes

407) Blue Moonlight

408) Barbara Eden

409) The Darlings

410) Opie Taylor

411) What is the password at the Regal Order of the Golden Door to Good Fellowship?

412) What is the name of Helen Crump's niece?

413) Whom does Charlene Darling marry?

414) Who "declares" for Aunt Bee?

415) How many chin-ups does Ernest T. Bass claim he can do?

416) How many stoplights does Mayberry have?

417) What flower is Andy a "giant" at potting?

418) What flower does Opie destroy with a football?

419) What is Daphne's catch phrase greeting?

420) What prize do Mayberry boys hope to win by selling Miracle Salve?

421) Who gives Aunt Bee a mustache cup?

422) Whose car does Floyd consider buying?

411) Geronimo

412) Cynthia

413) Dud Wash

414) Briscoe Darling

415) Eighteen

416) One (that we know of)

417) Petunias

418) A rose

419) "Hello, Doll!"

420) A pony

421) Mr. Frisby

422) Gilly Walker's

423) What public office does Ellie Walker run for?

424) What does Goober think is special about his dog?

425) Besides Helen (and his late wife), to whom does Andy knowingly propose marriage?

426) Who sang "Ol' Dan Tucker?"

427) What woman do Andy and Barney describe as "nice?"

428) Who finds a briefcase full of money near the railroad tracks?

429) What does "bully" Steve Quincy break with an apple?

430) What relative does Barney frisk at a roadblock?

431) Who withdraws her life savings to get married?

432) What is Mr. Meldrim the president of?

433) What does Gomer buy Mary Grace so she won't be unadorned?

434) Who is mayor of Greendale?

435) What does Fletch bring to the boys on their camping trip?

436) Who is Aunt Bee's best friend?

437) Who uses his feet to solve math problems?

423) City Council

424) He can talk

425) Ellie Walker

426) Opie & Andy

427) Mary Grace Gossage

428) Barney

429) A streetlight

430) His mother

431) Mrs. Mendelbright

432) The Mayberry Security Bank

433) A corsage

434) Mayor Purdy

435) Archery equipment

436) Clara Edwards

437) Ernest T. Bass

438) Who removes the hinge pins to get Otis out of jail?

439) Where is Barney's Cousin Virgil from?

440) Who is the telephone lineman that Andy thinks Opie invented?

441) Who says "you people are living in another world!"?

442) How many women hold Barney and Floyd hostage?

443) How many times does prisoner Dan Caldwell pull the trigger on Barney's gun?

444) What is Mrs. Magruder's occupation?

445) What two main characters have red (not auburn) hair?

446) What does Earl Pike buy his 57-year-old son for his birthday?

447) What official gets drunk and passes out in the courthouse?

448) Who is forced to wear a bucket on his head to help him think more clearly?

449) Name the umpire who calls Opie out at home plate.

450) Who is the "gentleman" prisoner?

438) Cousin Virgil

439) New Jersey

440) Mr. McBeevee

441) Malcolm Tucker

442) Three

443) Five

444) Cleaning lady

445) Opie and Thelma Lou

446) A car

447) Mayor Stoner

448) Gomer

449) Andy

450) Dan Caldwell

451) What makes Barney's "bloodhound" attack?

452) Who doesn't like to "chit-chat?"

453) Who or what is Eagle-Eye Annie?

454) Who wins a doll at the County Fair shooting gallery?

455) To what movie star does the lady speeder say Barney bears a striking resemblance?

456) Name one of the Taylor's butter and egg men.

457) What is the "miracle" drug Emma Watson takes?

458) How many wishes, in total, are apparently granted by Count Istvan Telecki?

459) What city celebrates "Mayberry Days" the last weekend in September every year?

460) What is Emmett's Brother-In-Law's line of work?

461) Who threatens to beat up Howard?

462) Whose house is Barney's first choice to hold the summit meeting?

463) What does Opie like to hide under the pillow on his bed?

464) Who played Opie's administrative assistant in the movie Back to Mayberry?

451) A dog whistle

452) Lydia Crosswaithe

453) Andy's fishing pole

454) Goober

455) Frank Sinatra

456) Orville Hendricks, Thurston, or Mr. Frisby

457) Sugar pills

458) Four (Three for Opie, One for Barney, One for Helen)

459) Mount Airy, North Carolina

460) Insurance Sales

461) Clyde Plot

462) Mr. McCabe's

463) Food

464) Karen Knotts

465) Who dated a librarian?

466) Who wore a toupee once to try and look younger?

467) What does the escaped prisoner smell that Andy is cooking at his campsite?

468) What drink does Aunt Bee bring to Mr. Wheeler who has been "working on the hot roof?"

469) Barney says he can't eat when he has what physical condition?

470) What operation does the new doctor in town perform on Opie?

471) What does Thelma Lou's first husband do for a living?

472) From whom does Aunt Bee buy a car?

473) Who gives Aunt Bee driving lessons?

474) What meal does Andy eat three times in one night due to a communication problem with Goober?

475) What California family owned Floyd's barbershop?

476) What town is identified on the bus that brings Dud Wash back to Mayberry?

477) What flower did Charlene give Dud before he "went off to fulfill his country's needs?"

465) Howard

466) Emmett

467) Bacon

468) Lemonade

469) Hiccups

470) Tonsillectomy

471) Foreman on a wrecking crew

472) Goober

473) Goober

474) Dinner (spaghetti)

475) The Robinsons

476) Macon

477) A mountain gladiola

478) What institute of higher learning did Howard Sprague attend?

479) What is Helen Crump's occupation?

480) From the street, the courthouse door on the right has a sign that reads what?

481) Who is famous for throwing rocks through windows?

482) What Mayberrian is a descendent of a Revolutionary War Hero?

483) Who credits Andy with saving his life by putting out a fire?

484) Who claims his bicycle was stolen?

485) Who was Sheriff immediately prior to Andy?

486) Who receives a special award for learning?

487) What does Barney receive in commemoration of five years of service?

488) Who owned a Hudson Terraplane?

489) Who gave Barney a book to ward off bad luck?

490) What is Tillie Beggs' nickname?

491) Whose mother curls her hair with cardboard?

478) Bradbury Business College

479) Schoolteacher

480) Justice of the Peace

481) Ernest T. Bass

482) Otis Campbell

483) Gomer

484) Emmett

485) Sheriff Buckley

486) Ernest T. Bass

487) A watch

488) Barney's uncle

489) His grandmother

490) The Beaver

491) Sally Tums'

492) What does Andy tell Barney he and Karen Moore did after they had coffee?

493) Name two of the characters in the radio soap opera Aunt Bee follows.

494) What is the name of Otis' brother?

495) What business name does Floyd use when corresponding to Madeline Grayson?

496) How much does Opie charge his friends to see Barney "hanging himself "in Opie's house?

497) What does Barney consider buying from Newton Monroe prior to his purchase of a fur piece?

498) What is the name of the runaway boy who visits the Taylors?

499) What does Gomer say is the cost per "ding" for gasoline?

500) Who tries to put shoes on an angry bull?

492) They got married

493) Celia, John, and Beverly

494) Ralph Campbell

495) Floyd Lawson Enterprises

496) Five cents

497) A pencil sharpener

498) George Foley

499) 30 cents

500) Luke Jenson

MULTIPLE CHOICE

1) According to Ernest T. Bass, how can you catch a duck if it is standing still?
   a) By the bill
   b) By the tail
   c) Hypnotize it
   d) Sing to it

2) Which of the following will NOT get Goober to leave his post inside the Courthouse?
   a) Fire
   b) Famine
   c) Flood
   d) Going to the drug store to get a sandwich

3) Who was Valedictorian of Mayberry Union High in 1945?
   a) Egbert Rollins
   b) Warren Ferguson
   c) Andy Taylor
   d) Thelma Lou

4) What is Barney's position in the Mayberry Band?
   a) Drummer
   b) Saxophone
   c) Harmonica
   d) Standby cymbalist

5) Andy tells Opie there are two kinds of people in this world:
   a) Winners and losers
   b) Givers and takers
   c) Haves and Have nots
   d) Men and women

1) By the bill

2) Flood

3) Andy Taylor

4) Standby cymbalist

5) Givers and takers

6) Who actually sings Barney's solo in "Good ol' 14-A"?
   a) Andy
   b) Glenn Cripe
   c) Jim Lindsey
   d) Bobbie Pruitt

7) What kind of soup does Andy consider delicious when it is done right?
   a) Lentil
   b) Chicken Noodle
   c) Minestrone
   d) Black bean

8) How many daughters does Mayor Pike have?
   a) Three
   b) Four
   c) Five
   d) Six

9) What is the first name of Mayor Pike's third daughter?
   a) Jezebel
   b) Rita
   c) Jenny
   d) Josephine

10) What two people sing "Sweet Adeline" into Barney's tape recorder?
    a) Gomer and Andy
    b) Andy and Barney
    c) Barney and Otis
    d) Otis and Jed

6) Glenn Cripe

7) Minestrone

8) Three

9) Josephine

10) Barney and Otis

11) Who taught Barney and Andy biology in school?
    a) Mr. Hamburger
    b) Mrs. Webster
    c) Mr. Schlemp
    d) Old lady McGruder

12) Who plays the saxophone in the Mayberry band?
    a) Barney
    b) Andy
    c) Luther
    d) Floyd

13) Where was the old Cascade club?

    a) Toledo
    b) Cleveland
    c) Cincinnati
    d) Akron

14) According to Barney, who gets a bargain at Weaver's department store?
    a) Nobody
    b) Aunt Bee
    c) Clara Edwards
    d) Floyd

15) By which name is Andy never referred to?
    a) Sheriff of Nottingham
    b) Sheriff Trailer
    c) Sheriff Matt Dillon
    d) Mighty Sheriff of Mayberry

11) Mrs. Webster

12) Luther

13) Toledo

14) Nobody

15) Sheriff of Nottingham

16) According to Andy, what is the best way to fix a chicken lunch?
   a) Chicken a la king
   b) Chicken with crust
   c) Chicken sandwich
   d) Fried chicken

17) What slogan does Floyd put in his ad for the Founder's Day program?
   a) Two chairs, no waiting
   b) Fastest service in town
   c) Best clip joint in town
   d) Movie star looks

18) What is the fabric of Opie's suit that the Darling's give him?
   a) Tropical Worsted
   b) Genuine polyester
   c) Synthetic horsehair
   d) Dacron

19) What were the only two things that Danny Williams ate/drank from his meal in jail?
   a) Bread and water
   b) Chicken and dumplings
   c) Milk and cookies
   d) Milk and Apple pie

20) Who plays the saxophone in the Original Carl Benson and His Wildcats band?
   a) Carl Benson
   b) Carl's mother
   c) Carl's 2nd cousin
   d) Carl's wife

16) Chicken with crust

17) Best clip joint in town

18) Tropical Worsted

19) Bread and water

20) Carl's mother

21) Who is NOT a member of the Mayberry
knot tying club?
    a) Barney
    b) Floyd
    c) Otis
    d) Gomer

22) How many Emmy awards did the cast of The Andy Griffith
Show win for their work on the series?
    a) Zero
    b) One
    c) Three
    d) Six

23) What is Darlene Swanson voted most likely to do at Miss
Wellington's School for Girls?
    a) Most likely to become charming
    b) Most likely to succeed
    c) Most likely to get married
    d) Most likely to move out of town

24) What does Mrs. Mendelbright receive for being the most
faithful member at church?
    a) A White Bible
    b) A plaque
    c) A magazine subscription
    d) A statue

25) What is the fine or penalty in Mayberry for public
intoxication?
    a) 2 days in jail
    b) $10 or 10 days in jail
    c) $2 or 24 hours in jail
    d) No official fine

21) Floyd

22) Six

23) Most likely to become charming

24) A White Bible

25) $2 or 24 hours in jail

26) Who is the girl back home who accepts Jeff Pruitt for who he is?
   a) Gladys
   b) Thelma
   c) Raylene
   d) Bertha

27) On how many streets do Opie and Howie deliver their newspaper?
   a) Three
   b) Six
   c) Eight
   d) Fifteen

28) According to Aunt Bee, why did Rose Blake go to Raleigh?
   a) To look for a husband
   b) To buy a new set of teeth
   c) To buy a motorcycle
   d) To take a pinch of snuff

29) Who is distant kin of Mr. Foley?
   a) Otis
   b) Andy
   c) Floyd
   d) Lamar Tuttle

30) Who punched Floyd in the nose?
   a) Mr. Foley
   b) Goober
   c) Lamar Tuttle
   d) Otis

26) Bertha

27) Three

28) To buy a new set of teeth

29) Otis

30) Otis

31) According to Barney, what was better about the old school system?
    a) You grew up hating your teachers
    b) All grades in one classroom
    c) Teachers were ugly
    d) Longer school hours

32) How long does Barney cook Otis' eggs?
    a) Two minutes
    b) Four minutes
    c) Ten minutes
    d) Thirty minutes

33) Who is accused of stealing car batteries?
    a) Barney
    b) Newton Monroe
    c) Luke Jensen
    d) Jimmy Morgan

34) Who accuses a Mayberry resident of stealing car batteries?
    a) Andy
    b) Barney
    c) Mr. Parmaley
    d) Mr. Carter

35) How much time does Ernest T. Have to court Charlene before she is married?
    a) 24 hours
    b) The weekend
    c) 1 week
    d) 1 year

31) You grew up hating your teachers

32) Four minutes

33) Jimmy Morgan

34) Mr. Carter

35) 24 hours

36) Who traditionally plays Lady Mayberry in the Centennial Pageant?
   a) Aunt Bee
   b) Clara Edwards
   c) Rosie Jacobs
   d) Jenny Jacobs

37) Who is going to have a tough time analyzing Ernest T's rock since so many people touched it at Mrs. Wiley's party?
   a) Barney
   b) The Raleigh police
   c) The boys at the lab
   d) The FBI

38) Who does Barney say will draw a sketch to help identify the rock thrower at Mrs. Wiley's party?
   a) Barney
   b) The staff artist of the Sheriff's department
   c) Buzz Fluhart
   d) A hired professional

39) What do they check for during a shakedown at the Mayberry jail?
   a) Beds properly made
   b) Dirty magazines
   c) Guns and knives
   d) Moonshine

40) Where does Andy take Helen on their first date together?
   a) Myers Lake
   b) The Diner
   c) Miniature golf
   d) Mt. Pilot for Chinese

36) Clara Edwards

37) The boys at the lab

38) The staff artist of the Sheriff's department

39) Guns and knives

40) Mt. Pilot for Chinese

41) What is the real first name of Melissa Stevens, Barney's "fiancée"?
   a) Gladys
   b) Gertrude
   c) Jamie
   d) Emma

42) On which holiday did the town's cannon muzzle bust?
   a) Memorial Day
   b) Fourth of July
   c) Founders Day
   d) Seth Taylor Day

43) What is NOT one of Andy's other names for Colonel Harvey's Elixir?
   a) Hooch
   b) Booze
   c) Fire water
   d) Happy water

44) Which moonshiner has a fine singing voice?
   a) Big Jack Anderson
   b) Otis Campbell
   c) Rube Sloan
   d) Rafe Hollister

45) What flavor ice cream does Barney deliver to Thelma Lou?
   a) Huckleberry Delight
   b) West Indian Licorice Mocha Delight
   c) Three-bean
   d) Triple Fudge Swirl

41) Gladys

42) Fourth of July

43) Fire water

44) Rafe Hollister

45) West Indian Licorice Mocha Delight

46) How does Andy usually trim the hedges?
    a) With his nail clippers
    b) With a cycle
    c) Just lops off the tops
    d) Gives it an Indian motif

47) Who does Andy say has a high roof to his mouth?
    a) Opie
    b) Barney
    c) Rafe Hollister
    d) Gomer

48) What county is Myers Lake in?
    a) Stokes
    b) Mayberry
    c) Myer
    d) Siler

49) What would Howie Pruitt do if the lights went out?
    e) Scream
    f) Start a fire
    g) Put in a fuse
    h) Light a candle

50) Which magazine listed below does Barney read?
    a) Crime Fighters' Monthly
    b) Psychology Weekly
    c) True Blue Detective
    d) Unsolved Mysteries

51) What is Ellie Walker's uncle's name?
    a) Jim Walker
    b) Rube Walker
    c) Frank Walker
    d) Fred Walker

46) Just lops off the tops

47) Gomer

48) Stokes

49) Put in a fuse

50) True Blue Detective

51) Fred Walker

52) According to Barney, what does Thelma Lou do when she is feeling good?
   a) Hums
   b) Sings
   c) Laughs
   d) Whistles

53) Who answers the phone if you call 247?
   a) Juanita
   b) Thelma Lou
   c) Helen
   d) Barney

54) To whom does Andy sell the old town cannon?
   a) Ben Prichard
   b) Ralph Mason
   c) Harvey Martin
   d) Brent Robbins

55) Who operates a still at Furnace Creek?
   a) Otis
   b) Big Jack Anderson
   c) Rafe Hollister
   d) Rube Sloan

56) What business is Mayor Stoner's brother in?
   a) Runs a gas station
   b) Runs a construction company
   c) Sells farm equipment
   d) Runs a department store

52) Hums

53) Thelma Lou

54) Ralph Mason

55) Rube Sloan

56) Runs a gas station

57) How old does Barney claim his former teacher Mrs. Thicket was?
   a) 19
   b) 107
   c) 200
   d) A million years old

58) What detective firm offers Andy a job?
   a) Raleigh detectives
   b) Stealth detectives
   c) Hogarth detectives
   d) Ace detectives

59) Who employed Malcolm Merriweather as a "gentleman's gentleman?"
   a) Colonel Chumley
   b) King of England
   c) Lord Brumley
   d) Colonel Harvey

60) Who is starring in the movie Gomer wants to see rather than get "back to nature"?
   a) Preston Foster
   b) William Holden
   c) Clark Gable
   d) Rock Hudson

61) What does Opie get for free from Ellie Walker at the drug store?
   a) A sucker
   b) An ice cream cone
   c) Licorice
   d) A popsicle

57)   107

58)   Hogarth detectives

59)   Colonel Chumley

60)   Preston Foster

61)   An ice cream cone

62) What state is Thelma Lou's cousin Karen Moore from?
   a) Texas
   b) Missouri
   c) Arkansas
   d) Georgia

63) Who steers while Barney's broken-down car is pushed back to town?
   a) Opie
   b) Aunt Bee
   c) Gomer
   d) Thelma Lou

64) What is Cousin Virgil's father's occupation?
   a) Sculptor
   b) Cabinet maker
   c) Key maker
   d) Candlestick maker

65) What is the name of the record company that produces a folk album featuring Mayberry musicians?
   a) Horizon records
   b) National Records
   c) Country records
   d) Groovy tunes

66) What is found at the end of Willow Lane?
   a) Kelsey's woods
   b) Remshaw house
   c) The duck pond
   d) Myers Lake

62) Arkansas

63) Thelma Lou

64) Cabinet maker

65) National Records

66) The duck pond

67) What is Malcolm Merriweather's mode of transportation?
   a) Unicycle
   b) Car
   c) Walking
   d) Bicycle

68) Which room in the Taylor house has a crack in the ceiling?
   a) Kitchen
   b) Dining room
   c) Andy's bedroom
   d) Living room

69) How old is Andy's house when he shows it to the Sims'?
   a) 10 years
   b) 20 years
   c) 35 years
   d) 50 years

70) Who owned Andy's house before him?
   a) Old man Poindexter
   b) Old man Johnson
   c) Old man Henson
   d) Old man Parmaley

71) For what holiday was Floyd once deputized?
   a) Veterans' Day
   b) Memorial Day
   c) Founders' Day
   d) New Year's Day

67) Bicycle

68) Kitchen

69) 35 years

70) Old man Parmaley

71) Veterans' Day

72) Whom does Andy accuse of making a down payment on a husband?
   a) Aunt Bee
   b) Ellie Walker
   c) Emma Watson
   d) Helen Crump

73) What kind of pistol does Asa Breeney have?
   a) Cap pistol
   b) .38 revolver
   c) Teddy Roosevelt horse pistol
   d) Walther PPK

74) What does Asa Breeney collect in a ball?
   a) Yarn
   b) Shoe strings
   c) Gum
   d) Tin Foil

75) What is the name of Frank Myers' chicken?
   a) Bertha
   b) Gertrude
   c) Hazel
   d) Bo

76) Whose laundry does Barney take down when he borrows a dress to "rob the bank?"
   a) Clara Edward's
   b) Mrs. Kelsey's
   c) Aunt Bee's
   d) Mrs. McGruder's

72) Ellie Walker

73) Teddy Roosevelt horse pistol

74) Tin Foil

75) Hazel

76) Mrs. Kelsey's

77) Which night of the week does Annabelle Silby regularly spend dancing with war veterans?
    a) Friday
    b) Sunday
    c) Saturday
    d) Thursday

78) What does Andy say Ph.G. stands for on Ellie Walker's diploma?
    a) Pharmacy girl
    b) Phone gal
    c) Feel good
    d) Pharmacy gal

79) On which day of the week does Opie find $50?
    a) Wednesday
    b) Friday
    c) Saturday
    d) Sunday

80) What time of the day can Opie claim the $50 he finds if nobody claims it?
    a) Noon
    b) 3 p.m.
    c) 5 p.m.
    d) 6:15 p.m.

81) What is Sam Burton's vice?
    a) Gambling
    b) Smoking
    c) Womanizing
    d) Hits the sauce

77) Saturday

78) Pharmacy gal

79) Wednesday

80) 3 p.m.

81) Hits the sauce

82) How much money does Barney have in the bank before he buys his car from Mrs. Lesch?
   a) $100
   b) $200
   c) $250
   d) $300

83) What two items does the woman shoplifter have in her bag?
   a) Her knitting and a Bible
   b) Picture of the president and an ID bracelet
   c) Gun and knife
   d) Tear gas and whistle

84) What title does Andy suggest should be bestowed upon Aunt Bee for the fine lunches she prepares?
   a) Miss Mayberry Chef
   b) Miss Luncheon Tray
   c) Miss Calories
   d) Miss Good Eatin'

85) Where do Barney & Phoebe Gilbert go on a date?
   a) Morelli's
   b) The duck pond
   c) The Blue View
   d) The Gigolo club

86) What does Barney say a Cornish pasty looks like?
   a) A big ravioli
   b) A baked potato
   c) An oversized plum
   d) An egg roll

82) $300

83) Her knitting and a Bible

84) Miss Luncheon Tray

85) The Blue View

86) A big ravioli

87) According to Andy, what kind of pie was eaten by Burley Peters prior to the marching band demonstration?
   a) Blueberry
   b) Apple
   c) Peach
   d) Pecan

88) What ordinance requires a license to peddle door to door?
   a) The Great Mayberry Ordinance
   b) Green River Ordinance
   c) Ordinance 612
   d) The Glower Ordinance

89) According to Barney, what does anxiety do to fearsome objects?
   a) Makes them larger than life
   b) Shrinks them
   c) Magnifies them
   d) Makes them disappear

90) What of Barney's has never been successfully photographed?
   a) His quick draw
   b) His gun
   c) His temper
   d) His trigger finger

91) What type of poetry does Briscoe call the poem Aunt Bee recites in his presence?
   a) Rose poetry
   b) Honest poetry
   c) Poetry from the heart
   d) Heart to heart poetry

87) Blueberry

88) Green River Ordinance

89) Magnifies them

90) His quick draw

91) Rose poetry

92) What two movies cause Barney to worry that he'd have Opie's warped psyche on his hands?
    a) Fire Planet, Ghosts From The Depths
    b) House of Blood, The Beast That Ate Minnesota
    c) The Beast From Out Of Town, Night Terrors
    d) Dracula, The Bride Of Frankenstein

93) How many black and white episodes are there of The Andy Griffith Show?
    a) 50
    b) 101
    c) 159
    d) 233

94) What was Aunt Bee's greatest experience prior to meeting Colonel Harvey?
    a) Meeting the Pope
    b) Being baptized
    c) Playing queen in a school play
    d) Getting married

95) With what company does Jim Lindsey finance his red sports car?
    a) Raleigh Financing
    b) Mid-Mountain Finance Company
    c) Appalachian Finance Company
    d) Entertainer's Finance Company

96) What two things does Barney say Floyd can't move at the same time?
    a) His feet and his mouth
    b) His feet and his hands
    c) His scissors and his jawbone
    d) His car and his house

92) House of Blood, The Beast That Ate Minnesota

93) 159

94) Being baptized

95) Mid-Mountain Finance Company

96) His scissors and his jawbone

97) What is Otis' hobby?
   a) Stamp collecting
   b) Bottle collecting
   c) Trivia
   d) Drinking

98) In order to get to Florida, how much money does Roger Hanover ask to borrow from Andy?
   a) $400
   b) $50
   c) $250
   d) $1000

99) Who is the back-up manicurist at Floyd's?
   a) Emma Watson
   b) Helen Crump
   c) Bertha Johnson
   d) Mr. Meldrin

100) Where is Roger Hanover from?
   a) Siler city
   b) Miami
   c) Raleigh
   d) Greensboro

101) What railroad did Weary Willie claim he once worked for?
   a) Norfolk and Southern
   b) Penn Traffic
   c) Raleigh Railroad
   d) CB & Q railroad

97)   Drinking

98) $400

99)   Emma Watson

100) Raleigh

101) CB & Q railroad

102) Which night does Barney take Judo lessons?
    a) Thursday
    b) Friday
    c) Saturday
    d) Monday

103) What is Howard Sprague's beverage of choice at the lodge?
    a) A malted
    b) Root Beer
    c) Ginger ale
    d) A Shirley Temple

104) Who calls Andy a home wrecker?
    a) Briscoe Darling
    b) Charlene Darling
    c) Barney
    d) Dud Wash

105) What does Emma Watson say she does with peroxide?
    a) Uses it for her cat
    b) Buys it for a friend
    c) Colors her hair with it
    d) Gargles with it

106) What gift does Aunt Bee NOT receive on her nicest birthday ever?
    a) Baseball Cap
    b) A bed jacket
    c) 2 dozen preserve jars
    d) Salt & pepper shakers

102) Thursday

103) Root Beer

104) Dud Wash

105) Gargles with it

106) Baseball Cap

107) How much does Opie want to spend on a gift for Miss Crump?
   a) 25 cents
   b) 74 cents
   c) 1 dollar
   d) 2 dollars

108) What is City Statute 249-A section V?
   a) No sweeping into the street
   b) No loitering
   c) No bikes on the sidewalk
   d) No jaywalking

109) Where do you call when you dial 142-R?
   a) The Junction Café
   b) Walker's drug store
   c) The Sheriff's office
   d) Floyd's

110) When at the fishing hole what will you feel as fresh as?
   a) A lemonade
   b) A summer day
   c) A daisy
   d) A spring day

111) Who can make smoke come out of his ears?
   a) Colonel Harvey
   b) Mr. McBeevee
   c) Malcolm Merriweather
   d) Dr. Pendyke

112) What does Colonel Harvey's smoke signal mean?
   a) The British are coming
   b) Run for the hills
   c) The cavalry is coming
   d) The modem is down

107) 74 cents

108) No bikes on the sidewalk

109) The Junction Cafe

110) A lemonade

111) Mr. Mc Beevee

112) The cavalry is coming

113) What does Malcolm Merriweather call a "sheriff"?
    a) Policeman
    b) Law maker
    c) Constable
    d) Enforcer

114) What type of phone line does Barney have at home?
    a) Private line
    b) Four party line
    c) He has no phone
    d) Three party line

115) Name two people that climb a tree to escape a bear?
    a) Mayor Stoner and Jess
    b) Andy and Barney
    c) Mayor Pike and Otis
    d) Aunt Bee and Helen

116) What color is Otis' bathrobe at the jail?
    a) Purple with polka dots
    b) Blue
    c) Pink
    d) Orange

117) What happens when Rafe Hollister greases his shoes?
    a) His wife hits him
    b) It smells up the joint
    c) The cats follow him
    d) The pigs come running

118) How much does Fred Plummer pay as a fine for sweeping trash into the street?
    a) Nothing
    b) 4 dollars
    c) 10 dollars
    d) 15 dollars

113) Constable

114) Three party line

115) Mayor Stoner and Jess

116) Blue

117) The cats follow him

118) 4 dollars

119) Where is the photo lab in Mayberry?
   a) Mrs. Mason's drugstore
   b) Walker's drugstore
   c) Franklyn pharmacy
   d) The dry cleaners

120) Who was one of the first Lawsons to settle in Mayberry?
   a) Seth Lawson
   b) James Lawson
   c) Daniel Lawson
   d) Carl Lawson

121) What side of town smells the landfill first? (N/S/E/W)
   a) North
   b) South
   c) East
   d) West

122) What is the student rate for an issue of Opie & Howie's newspaper?
   a) 10 cents
   b) 5 cents
   c) 2 cents
   d) 1 cent

123) What does Barney receive for being an outstanding performer in the Mayberry choir?
   a) A $10 merchandise certificate
   b) Two free haircuts
   c) Singing lessons
   d) Five lbs. of beef

119) Mrs. Mason's drugstore

120) Daniel Lawson

121) North

122) One cent

123) A $10 merchandise certificate

124) What magazine publishes the article "Sheriff Without a Gun"?
   a) True Blue Detective
   b) Law and Order
   c) Crime Wave
   d) Public Order

125) Why wasn't Barney scared at the mummy show?
   a) He is fearless Fife
   b) His mother wasn't scared
   c) He had his eyes closed
   d) He was overwhelmed by Brendan Fraser's Oscar-caliber performance

126) What song is sung by both Andy and Charlene, but in different episodes?
   a) There is a Time
   b) Dooley
   c) Dirty Me, Dirty Me
   d) Old Luke Walker

127) How long does Barney consider not washing the hand that shook the governor's hand?
   a) A week
   b) The rest of the day
   c) The weekend
   d) A month

128) Why do Barney & Floyd run out of gas when they end up at O'Malley's cabin?
   a) The gas line broke
   b) They took the shortcut
   c) Clogged fuel line
   d) Fuel gauge was broken

124) Law and Order

125) He had his eyes closed

126) There is a Time

127) A week

128) They took the shortcut

129) How often does Morelli's change their tablecloths?
   a) Hourly
   b) Weekly
   c) Daily
   d) Bi-weekly

130) How much is J. Howard Jackson's fine for speeding and failure to report to court?
   a) $5
   b) $10
   c) $15
   d) $25

131) How much does Naomi Conners (the female convict) weigh?
   a) 115 lbs.
   b) 99 lbs.
   c) 151 lbs.
   d) 200 lbs.

132) What dance does Barney wait for all year?
   a) Founders day dance
   b) Chamber of Commerce dance
   c) Mayberry square dance
   d) Raleigh-Mayberry dance

133) What can't carry Andy and Peggy off if they hold onto each other?
   a) The wind
   b) A big fish
   c) A hawk
   d) A mosquito

129) Daily

130) $15

131) 115 lbs

132) Chamber of Commerce dance

133) A hawk

134) What doctor is out of town when Andy delivers Sam Becker's child?
   a) Doc Johnson
   b) Doc Winters
   c) Doc Andrews
   d) Doc Stevens

135) What is a 42 – J which Barney wants to run on Aunt Bee's boyfriend?
   a) Character report
   b) Credit report
   c) Criminal record report
   d) Stolen car report

136) For what holiday is Goober always deputized?
   a) Memorial Day
   b) Halloween
   c) Founders' Day
   d) Labor Day

137) What vegetable is found in the back of Ron Bailey's car?
   a) Corn
   b) Tomatoes
   c) Celery
   d) Squash

138) What item does Opie NOT bring to Mr. McBeevee?
   a) Spring water
   b) Carrots
   c) Berries
   d) Apples

134) Doc Winters

135) Character report

136) Halloween

137) Celery

138) Carrots

139) How many years did Andy teach Sunday School before being hog-tied into another month of Sunday's
    a) Three years
    b) One year
    c) Seven years
    d) Ten years

140) Why does Andy like Floyd to cut his hair before lunch?
    a) Floyd has an "early bird" discount
    b) Floyd may have onions for lunch
    c) Floyd isn't jittery from coffee
    d) Floyd is awake

141) Where did O'Malley get his money?
    a) Won it
    b) Married into it
    c) Inherited it
    d) Found it

142) Who was the bully who tried to get Andy's fishing spot as a boy?
    a) Billy Cartwright
    b) Jesse Williams
    c) Hodie Snitch
    d) Buddy Bully

143) According to Barney, how many reflectors do rich kids have on their bicycles?
    a) 1-2
    b) 3-4
    c) Rich kids don't need any
    d) 6 or 7

139) Three years

140) Floyd may have onions for lunch

141) Married into it

142) Hodie Snitch

143) 6 or 7

144) How much is the steak sandwich dinner at the Diner?
   a) $1.25
   b) $.99
   c) $1.99
   d) $2.25

145) How much was the bet between Gomer and Birdie to find a trout in that pool?
   a) 5 cents
   b) 30 cents
   c) $1.00
   d) 95 cents

146) How does Barney say Andy & Helen can use the money they save on a quickie wedding?
   a) Furniture
   b) A house
   c) A car
   d) Baby needs

147) Why did it take Mayberry so long to get blacktop at the gasworks?
   a) Regis was picketing it
   b) Fear of a plague
   c) Asphalt shortage
   d) They were slow in getting federal aid

148) Who placed 1st and 2nd in the County Penmanship competition?
   a) Andy and Barney
   b) Aunt Bee and Clara Edwards
   c) Opie and Howie
   d) Goober and Gomer

144) $1.25

145) 30 cents

146) Furniture

147) They were slow in getting federal aid

148) Andy and Barney

149) What was the highest rated TV movie in 1986?
    a) Earthquake
    b) Return to Mayberry
    c) Escape from Alcatraz
    d) Get Smart

150) What are the green things in Asa's gun belt?
    a) Bullets
    b) Tin foil
    c) Marbles
    d) Pennies

151) Why does Barney object to the stamp machine in the Post Office?
    a) It doesn't give change
    b) Kids play with it
    c) It eats his money
    d) U.S. government shouldn't be transacting business through a slot machine

152) Who operates a still at Council Flats?
    a) Ben Sewell
    b) Big Jack Anderson
    c) Otis
    d) Rafe Hollister

153) How does Gilly Walker aim to drive?
    a) Slow, every now and then
    b) Foolishly
    c) Reckless
    d) Fast

149) Return to Mayberry

150) Bullets

151) U.S. government shouldn't be transacting business through a slot machine

152) Ben Sewell

153) Fast

154) Who is Virginia Lee's uncle?
   a) Andy
   b) Howard Sprague
   c) Floyd Lawson
   d) Barney

155) How many years in a row had Andy & Barney won the opening day fishing sweepstakes?
   a) 2 years
   b) 6 years
   c) 10 years
   d) 3 years

156) Whose wife comes out on a horse and sings that opera stuff?
   a) Mayor Pike's
   b) Mayor Stoner's
   c) George Koontz's
   d) Billy Egbert's

157) What town did Frances Bavier retire to?
   a) Raleigh, North Carolina
   b) Siler City, North Carolina
   c) Pilot Mountain, North Carolina
   d) Wheeling, West Virginia

158) What do Mr. Foley and Otis have in common?
   a) They are cousins
   b) They both have a wife named Rita
   c) Each is hit by a tomato during an episode
   d) Each slips and falls down during an episode

159) What does Steve Quincy say is for sissies?
   a) Fishing
   b) Baseball
   c) School

154) Floyd Lawson

155) 3 years

156) Mayor Pike's

157) Siler City, North Carolina

158) Each is hit by a tomato during an episode

159) Fishing

160) Frank Myers claims to have a medallion for the St. Louis World's Fair from which year?
   a) 1906
   b) 1929
   c) 1939
   d) 1952

161) What does Mr. Schwamp try to do to Ernest T. Bass at Mrs. Wiley's party?
   a) Tackle him
   b) Pinch him
   c) Talk to him
   d) Dance with him

162) What part did Don Knotts play in the movie Pleasantville?
   a) A deputy sheriff
   b) A gas station attendant
   c) A TV repairman
   d) A lawyer

163) What is the name of the last wild bird Opie lets go from the cage?
   a) Nod
   b) Wynken
   c) Blynken
   d) McCartney

164) What does Daphne want to play with the sheriff?
   a) Prisoner
   b) Chase
   c) Checkers
   d) Big House

160) 1906

161) Pinch him

162) A TV repairman

163) Blynken

164) Big House

165) What does Barney give to Opie to help him feed his wild birds?
   a) Eye dropper
   b) Gloves
   c) Goggles
   d) Tweezers

166) What does Thelma Lou ask Lillian to bring to the party in hopes that she won't bring meatballs?
   a) Dip
   b) Rolls
   c) Punch
   d) Balloons

167) How many apples does Opie trade to get a can to kick?
   a) Two
   b) A dozen
   c) Eight
   d) Twenty-four

168) It's bad luck to look over a man's left shoulder when he is doing this?
   a) Playing horseshoes
   b) Playing guitar
   c) Playing cards
   d) Playing checkers

169) Which game does Barney NOT play against himself?
   a) Parcheesi
   b) Checkers
   c) Casino
   d) Poker

165) Tweezers

166) Rolls

167) Eight

168) Playing checkers

169) Poker

170) What does Ernest T. love more than his cow and his .22 repeater?
   a) His possum
   b) His sweet Romeena
   c) His gold tooth
   d) Apple pie

171) Name the bully who extorts milk money from Opie.
   a) Russell
   b) Billy
   c) Sheldon
   d) Wilton

172) In what city does Lydia Crosswaithe work?
   a) Greensboro
   b) Siler City
   c) Elm City
   d) Mt. Pilot

173) How many color episodes of The Andy Griffith Show were made?
   a) Ninety
   b) Sixty-two
   c) Eighty
   d) Forty- five

174) From what city did the bookie barber retire?
   a) Cleveland
   b) Raleigh
   c) Siler City
   d) Chicago

170) His sweet Romeena

171) Sheldon

172) Mt. Pilot

173) Ninety

174) Raleigh

175) Who always wins the sack race at the church picnic?
   a) Goober
   b) Jim Lindsey
   c) Jim Summers
   d) Willie Juniper

176) What job does Barney consider taking at the pickle factory?
   a) Brine tester
   b) Canner
   c) Plucker
   d) Squeezer

177) What is the fine Bobby Fleet incurs for robe dignity offending?
   a) $50
   b) $10
   c) $25
   d) $100

178) What one thing do prisoners NOT get in the big house?
   a) One cot
   b) One blanket
   c) One book
   d) One cracked mirror

179) What does M.D. stand for in Barney Fife, M.D?
   a) Medical doctor
   b) Maniac deputy
   c) Mayberry deputy
   d) Mystery deputy

180) What have you done if you've violated Rule 8, section B?
   a) Loitered
   b) Gossiped
   c) Peddled door-to-door
   d) Parked too close to a fire hydrant

175) Jim Summers

176) Brine tester

177) $50

178) One book

179) Mayberry Deputy

180) Parked too close to a fire hydrant

181) What is the minimum number of footsteps you can park from a fire hydrant?
   a) 5
   b) 8 and ½
   c) 11
   d) 3

182) How many good laying hens is the owner of a crushed 1949 Hudson Terraplane requesting in exchange for his car?
   a) 6
   b) 12
   c) 24
   d) 36

183) What store does Ben Weaver think is trying to get a foothold in Mayberry?
   a) Foster's
   b) Bert Miller's
   c) Steven's Department Store
   d) Bigg's

184) Under what condition does Otis NOT trust his own judgment?
   a) Early in the morning
   b) Late at night
   c) Under stress
   d) When he is sober

185) If Floyd has a cup of coffee for breakfast, what time does he like to have a 2nd cup?
   a) 10 am
   b) Noon
   c) 2 pm
   d) 4 pm

181) 8 and ½

182) 12

183) Steven's Department Store

184) When he is sober

185) 10 am

186) What gift does Elizabeth Crowley, the female speeder, give to Opie?
   a) Bicycle
   b) Autographed Baseball
   c) Basketball
   d) A picture of Johnny Unitas

187) What routine check does Andy want to hold Bobby Fleet's bus for?
   a) Bald tire check
   b) Carburetor check
   c) Interstate Pest Control
   d) Steering wheel control check

188) What type of pillow does Uncle Ollie use?
   a) Satin
   b) Extra fluffy
   c) Goose down
   d) Flat

189) What is NOT one of Big Maude Tyler's aliases?
   a) Annabelle Tyler
   b) John Henderson
   c) Maude Clarice Tyler
   d) Clarice Tyler

190) Whose naked photo is seen in one episode?
   a) Barney's
   b) Howard's
   c) Andy's
   d) Opie's

186) Autographed Baseball

187) Interstate Pest Control

188) Goose down

189) John Henderson

190) Andy's

191) Who is Aunt Bee's sister?
   a) Jenny
   b) Ruthie
   c) Margaret
   d) Nora

192) What two animals has Ernest T. Bass lived with?
   a) Possum and raccoon
   b) Gopher and chipmunk
   c) Skunk and mockingbird
   d) Wolf and cow

193) What one thing does Ernest T. Bass NOT do to make himself attractive to Romeena?
   a) Shaved the back of his neck
   b) Did 16 chin-ups
   c) Got a gold tooth
   d) Got an education

194) What does Goober win at the carnival shooting gallery?
   a) Razor
   b) Coffee
   c) Celluloid kewpie doll
   d) Pineapple skinner

195) What activity does Karen Folker consider to be un-ladylike?
   a) Doing cartwheels
   b) Standing on your head
   c) Burping
   d) Shouting

196) What flavor ice cream does Thelma Lou make for Opie?
   a) Peach
   b) Vanilla
   c) Butterscotch
   d) Chocolate

191) Nora

192) Possum and raccoon

193) Did 18 chin-ups

194) Celluloid kewpie doll

195) Standing on your head

196) Peach

197) According to Andy, what warning is printed on the label of Barney's cologne?
   a) Drives women wild
   b) User should wear gloves
   c) Use only under adult supervision
   d) Flammable

198) Why was Vicky Harmes all stuck up?
   a) She was prom queen
   b) Her daddy was in the Civil Service
   c) She had long blond hair
   d) Her teeth were capped

199) What state does a jar of pickles go to as a "safe driving award"?
   a) Texas
   b) New Mexico
   c) Oregon
   d) Indiana

200) After the initial seating assignment in Barney's new car, which two people change places prior to leaving?
   a) Andy and Thelma Lou
   b) Aunt Bee and Opie
   c) Opie and Gomer
   d) Andy and Gomer

201) Where did Barney first meet Vicky Harmes?
   a) On Main Street
   b) At the Chamber of Commerce dance
   c) Outside the ice cream parlor
   d) On the playground

197) User should wear gloves

198) Her daddy was in the Civil Service

199) Oregon

200) Opie and Gomer

201) Outside the ice cream parlor

202) Name the two prisoners who experience Barney's shakedown?
    a) Ralph and Gordon
    b) Bugsy and Ned
    c) The Johnson Brothers
    d) Tiny and Doc

203) What news service does "Joe Layton" claim to work for?
    a) Intercontinental News
    b) Raleigh Times
    c) Mayberry Gazette
    d) U.S. Times

204) Besides the gas station, where else did Goober once work?
    a) The Bluebird Diner
    b) Weaver's Department Store
    c) Boysinger's Bakery
    d) The Feed and Grain

205) From whom did Mr. McBeevee learn to make smoke come out of his ears?
    a) The Shawnee Indians
    b) The pirates
    c) The heathen cannibals
    d) Chimney sweeps

206) What does C.J. Hoffman claim to do for a living?
    a) Reporter
    b) Photographer
    c) Owns a magazine
    d) Owns a newspaper

202) Tiny and Doc

203) Intercontinental News

204) Weaver's Department Store

205) The heathen cannibals

206) Owns a newspaper

207) Who does Sheriff Mitchell say is handy with the ladies?
    a) Henry Wheeler
    b) Doug Brown
    c) Gentleman Dan Caldwell
    d) Barney

208) What thing does Gomer NOT do to repay Andy "the lifesaver man"?
    a) Chops wood
    b) Washes the courthouse windows
    c) Catches fresh fish
    d) Tunes up his car

209) Who is Floyd's best advertisement?
    a) Andy
    b) Goober
    c) Barney
    d) Howard Sprague

210) What item does Barney tell Aunt Bee he had sent to the cleaners?
    a) His shoes
    b) His razor
    c) His suitcase
    d) His wig

211) Who is hot copy for readers in the fifth grade?
    a) Jenny Walker
    b) Sally Tums
    c) Helen Crump
    d) Karen Folker

207) Henry Wheeler

208) Tunes up his car

209) Barney

210) His suitcase

211) Karen Folker

212) What type of cell can't Otis sleep in?
    a) A cold cell
    b) A strange cell
    c) A neat cell
    d) A dark cell

213) According to Barney, what means there's going to be a death in the family?
    a) Leaving the porch light on all night
    b) Seeing an owl in daylight
    c) A bird in the house
    d) Losing a four-leaf clover

214) According to Andy, you can change the name of a rose, but you can't do what?
    a) You can't change it into an orchid
    b) You can't grab it with your bare hands
    c) You can't do nothing about the smell
    d) You can't keep it alive forever

215) Who causes damage to Fletch Roberts' truck?
    a) Ronald Bailey
    b) Goober
    c) Floyd
    d) Malcolm Merriweather

216) According to Barney, what two places is Mayberry the gateway to?
    a) Crime & gambling
    b) Danger & Monte Carlo
    c) Fun and entertainment
    d) Heaven & Hell

212) A strange cell

213) A bird in the house

214) You can't do nothing about the smell

215) Malcolm Merriweather

216) Danger & Monte Carlo

217) According to Ernest T., which rodent has love all figured out?
   a) Possum
   b) Squirrel
   c) Muskrat
   d) Rat

218) At what time are Barney and Juanita going to see the drive-in movie in their uniforms?
   a) 6 p.m.
   b) 7:30 p.m.
   c) 8 p.m.
   d) 9:30 p.m.

219) Which of the following names does Eleanora Poultice suggest for the singing trio of Andy, Barney and Gomer?
   a) The Three Bells
   b) The Mayberry Three
   c) Four's a Crowd
   d) The Tops

220) Who does Barney replace in the town choir?
   a) Glen Cripes
   b) Ralph Pritchard
   c) Gomer
   d) Andy

221) What laundry service does Aunt Bee use?
   a) Quick Clean
   b) Jerry's
   c) Roy's
   d) Laundry-rite

217) Muskrat

218) 7:30 p.m.

219) The Three Bells

220) Ralph Pritchard

221) Roy's

222) Who robs the furniture factory payroll?
    a) Doc and Tiny
    b) Doc Malloy and his partner
    c) Eddie Blake
    d) Luke Comstock

223) How much do Andy and Barney tip Olive at the diner for her good service?
    a) 25 cents
    b) 50 cents
    c) 75 cents
    d) 1 dollar

224) What do Thelma Lou and Edgar Coleman do together?
    a) Dance
    b) Study poetry
    c) Glue covers back on hymnbooks
    d) Volunteer at the hospital

225) What species did Dr. Pendyke's veterinary practice NOT specialize in?
    a) Cats
    b) Birds
    c) Small sheep
    d) Cows

226) Where did Andy Griffith's father work in Mt. Airy, North Carolina?
    a) Sheriff's office
    b) Post office
    c) Furniture factory
    d) Paper mill

222) Doc Malloy and his partner

223) 50 cents

224) Glue covers back on hymnbooks

225) Cows

226) Furniture factory

227) Who showed Andy how to shoot his first .22 rifle?
   a) His Uncle Ollie
   b) His father
   c) His mother
   d) His brother Johnny

228) What song is #12 in the Mayberry Band's brown book?
   a) Battle Hymn of the Republic
   b) Our Lady of Mayberry
   c) Stars and Stripes Forever
   d) Old Brown Shoe

229) What war does Ms. Vickers think is still going on?
   a) WW I
   b) WW II
   c) Korean War
   d) Civil War

230) Which is NOT a reason Mayberry is crime free, according to Barney?
   a) Andy
   b) Barney
   c) Respect of the people
   d) Barney's gun

231) Who is NOT a real estate salesman in Mayberry?
   a) Mr. Shlummer
   b) Harry Walker
   c) Barney Fife
   d) Mr. Schwamp

227) His Uncle Ollie

228) Stars and Stripes Forever

229) Civil War

230) Respect of the people

231) Mr. Schwamp

232) What city does Ms. Vickers fear is in danger of being lost to the enemy?
   a) Washington, DC
   b) Richmond
   c) Atlanta
   d) New Orleans

233) In which season was The Andy Griffith Show rated #1 in the Neilson rating?
   a) 1st season
   b) 3rd season
   c) 5th season
   d) 8th and final season

234) Barney asks the Hollywood movie producer if he knows which movie star?
   a) Roc Hudson
   b) Gabby Hayes
   c) Bing Crosby
   d) Bob Hope

235) 235. Who has NOT been a sheriff of Mayberry?
   a) Sheriff Paley
   b) Sheriff Poindexter
   c) Sheriff Pinkley
   d) Sheriff Williams

236) Who is NOT mentioned in "The Ballad of Andy and Barney"?
   a) Dillinger
   b) Pretty Boy Floyd
   c) Al Capone
   d) Jesse James

232) Richmond

233) 8th and final season

234) Gabby Hayes

235) Sheriff Williams

236) Jesse James

237) What night is NOT a part of Barney and Thelma Lou's "routine"?
a) Monday
b) Tuesday
c) Thursday
d) Friday

238) Which is NOT one of Barney's trick shots with a slingshot?
a) Tailgunner
b) Over the creek
c) Under the bridge
d) Behind the barn

239) Who do many consider "the master of Mayberry trivia"?
a) Duke Slater
b) Fred Ziffel
c) Paul Mulik
d) Oliver Wendell Douglass

240) When living in Raleigh, Barney lives in a boarding house run by what family?
a) The Jensons
b) The Parkers
c) The Silbys
d) The Joneses

241) On what charge does Andy arrest Jim Lindsey as a pretense to introduce him to Bobby Fleet?
a) Disturbing the Peace
b) Resisting Arrest
c) Loitering
d) Not paying his bills

237) Monday

238) Over the creek

239) Paul Mulik

240) The Parkers

241) Resisting Arrest

242) Karen Moore beat Andy in:
   a) Checkers
   b) Fishing tournament
   c) Skeet shooting competition
   d) Chess

243) Name the sister and brother-in-law of Aunt Bee's who visits the Taylors:
   a) Gertrude and Same
   b) Millie and Orville
   c) Nora and Ollie
   d) Emma and Egbert

244) What street does Floyd live on?
   a) Maple
   b) Elm
   c) Willow
   d) Unknown

245) What does Goober buy when he accompanies Barney to an auction?
   a) Copper Tubing
   b) Tool Set
   c) Old Hub Caps
   d) Phonograph Records

246) Opie once wandered away from home and ate too many of what?
   a) Apples
   b) Strawberries
   c) Chocolates
   d) Candy Corns

242) Skeet shooting competition

243) Nora and Ollie

244) Unknown

245) Copper Tubing

246) Apples

247) What does Barney buy when he accompanies Goober to an auction?
   a) A Car
   b) A Fortune telling set
   c) A Gun
   d) A Tape Recorder

248) Who does Ernest T. Bass leave with after Mrs. Wiley's party?
   a) Ramona
   b) Thelma Lou
   c) Mary Grace
   d) Betty Lou

249) What does Mrs. Wiley call Ernest T. Bass?
   a) An Animal
   b) A Skunk
   c) A Baboon
   d) A Creature

250) What nickname does Barney use for Andy in the Centennial Play?
   a) Laughing Bull
   b) Laughing Face
   c) Happy Face
   d) Clown Face

251) What is the first prize that Opie wins at the County Fair shooting gallery?
   a) A Razor
   b) A Stuffed Animal
   c) A Wooden Donkey
   d) A Ceramic Pelican

247) A Fortune telling set

248) Ramona

249) A Creature

250) Laughing Face

251) A Ceramic Pelican

252) What is Mayor Stoner's first name?
   a) Ronald
   b) Roy
   c) Earl
   d) Gilly

253) What beverage does Andy order on his dinner date with Peggy in Raleigh?
   a) Milk
   b) Beer
   c) Tom Collins
   d) Seltzer Water

254) What does Andy call Barney when Barney wears his motorcycle clothes?
   a) Baron von Richthofen
   b) Baron von Zooter
   c) Baron von Roder
   d) The Red Baron

255) What illegal activity occurred at the Remshaw house?
   a) Gambling
   b) Counterfeiting
   c) Moonshining
   d) Drug Dealing

256) Who owns a #1 size chemistry set?
   a) Opie
   b) Howie
   c) Whitey
   d) Johnny Paul

252) Roy

253) Beer

254) Baron von Richthofen

255) Moonshining

256) Johnny Paul

257) Who does young Opie say "can't do anything"?
   a) Aunt Bee
   b) Barney
   c) Helen's Niece
   d) Floyd

258) Who does Jeff Pruitt call "little buddy"?
   a) Andy
   b) Barney
   c) Opie
   d) Goober

259) What item does Ben Weaver steal on Christmas Eve?
   a) A Car
   b) A Radio
   c) A Bench
   d) A Sign

260) Who calls Goober "power mad" because of his coaching style?
   a) Floyd
   b) Andy
   c) Barney
   d) Aunt Bee

261) How much money is Frank Meyer's bond supposedly worth?
   a) Over $250,000
   b) Over $300,000
   c) Over $500,000
   d) A Million Dollars

257) Aunt Bee

258) Barney

259) A Bench

260) Floyd

261) Over $300,000

262) What task does Henry Wheeler take care of for the Taylors?
    a) Fixes The Roof Shingles
    b) Sprays Rose Bushes
    c) Paints The House
    d) Mows The Lawn

263) Who tells Opie "If you touch a bird it will die"?
    a) Barney
    b) Johnny Paul
    c) Howie
    d) Goober

264) Who is NOT on the Mayberry bowling team?
    a) Howard
    b) Floyd
    c) Emmett
    d) Andy

265) Who banned Barney from the Philomathian Literary Society?
    a) Andy
    b) Clara Edwards
    c) Howard
    d) Jack Egbert

266) Who is the newspaper reporter covering the Mayberry vs. Mt. Pilot Little League baseball game?
    a) Barney
    b) Howard
    c) Goober
    d) Warren

262) Sprays Rose Bushes

263) Johnny Paul

264) Floyd

265) Jack Egbert

266) Howard

267) According to Andy, what is a police officer's most important piece of equipment?
    a) Badge
    b) Uniform
    c) Gun
    d) Squad Car

268) Who had a picture revealing that Opie was safe at the plate in the baseball game?
    a) Aunt Bee
    b) Helen
    c) Howard
    d) Floyd

269) Name the bakery where Millie works.
    a) Cupcake Crazy
    b) Mayberry Bakery
    c) Boysinger's Bakery
    d) Biggs Bakery

270) Whose cat did Andy think killed a songbird?
    a) Mrs. Snyder's
    b) Mrs. Edwards
    c) Mrs. Bellows
    d) Mr. Parmaley's

271) Which Deputy yawns during line-up?
    a) Goober
    b) Jed
    c) Floyd
    d) Otis

267) Badge

268) Helen

269) Boysinger's Bakery

270) Mrs. Snyder's

271) Jed

272) What was Barney's nickname when he won the 50 – yard dash as a youth?
    a) Barney The Rabbit
    b) Barney The Bullet
    c) Blazing Barney
    d) Fast Fife

273) Andy and Barney once tried to join what exclusive club?
    a) The Elks
    b) The Regal
    c) The Esquire
    d) The Pussycat

274) Who got their picture taken next to Malcolm Tucker's car?
    a) Goober
    b) Gomer
    c) Barney
    d) Andy

275) What day of the week does Malcolm Tucker's car break down outside Mayberry?
    a) Saturday
    b) Sunday
    c) Monday
    d) Friday

276) Who did Opie NOT have a crush on at some point?
    a) Helen
    b) Thelma Lou
    c) Karen
    d) Charlene Darling

272) Barney The Rabbit

273) The Esquire

274) Goober

275) Sunday

276) Charlene Darling

277) Which item that Newton Monroe sells in Mayberry is NOT seen?
   a) Wrist Watch
   b) Pineapple Skinner
   c) Transistor Radio
   d) Fur Piece

278) Whose brother owns a gas station in Mayberry?
   a) Mayor Stoner
   b) Goober
   c) Gomer
   d) Floyd

279) Who is Barney's landlady in Mayberry?
   a) His Mother
   b) Mrs. Watkins
   c) Mrs. Pendleton
   d) Mrs. Mendelbright

280) Who wrote a love note in Barney's school yearbook?
   a) Romona Wiley
   b) Sharon DeSpain
   c) Thelma Lou
   d) Helen Crump

281) Who does Goober say speaks like everybody else?
   a) Roc Hudson
   b) William Holden
   c) Cary Grant
   d) Glen Ford

277) Pineapple Skinner

278) Mayor Stoner

279) Mrs. Mendelbright

280) Romona Wiley

281) William Holden

282) What does Barney say must be causing all the hot weather in Mayberry?
   a) Climate Change
   b) Winds from Raleigh
   c) The Gypsies
   d) The Bomb

283) Opie once traded "licorice seeds" for what item?
   a) A Cap Pistol
   b) Roller Skates
   c) A Bent Penny
   d) A Bicycle

284) Who teaches Aunt Bee to drive?
   a) Andy
   b) Helen
   c) Howard
   d) Goober

285) What is the name of Andy and Barney's high school yearbook?
   a) Mayberry Memories
   b) Carolina Winds
   c) The Southerner
   d) The Cutlass

286) What does Andy buy from Newton Monroe?
   a) Napkins
   b) Nothing
   c) A Jack Knife
   d) A Tie

282) The Bomb

283) A Cap Pistol

284) Goober

285) The Cutlass

286) Nothing

287) Which of the following is NOT something Andy said he would wish for if he had a magic lamp?
   a) Socks
   b) Underwear
   c) Tennis Racket
   d) Basketball

288) How much does Barney pay for the fur piece he buys for Thelma Lou?
   a) $13.25
   b) $75.00
   c) $25.50
   d) $49.00

289) How long does Opie have to wait to claim the money he finds?
   a) 3 days
   b) 7 days
   c) 2 weeks
   d) 1 month

290) What does Mr. Darling say he needs in his hotel room?
   a) Bed and a bathroom
   b) Bed and a Bible
   c) Bed and a blanket
   d) Bed and some cider

291) Who is NOT one of the female escaped convicts?
   a) Sally
   b) Maude
   c) Macy
   d) Naomi

287) Tennis Racket

288) $13.25

289) 7 days

290) Bed and a Bible

291) Macy

292) Who does Barney compare to the Count of Monte Cristo?
   a) Ernest T. Bass
   b) Howard
   c) Gentleman Dan Caldwell
   d) Andy

293) The Taylors once baby- sat an infant who cried every time who held her?
   a) Opie
   b) Andy
   c) Aunt Bee
   d) Clara Edwards

294) What is Opie's favorite kind of cake?
   a) German Chocolate
   b) Chocolate
   c) Vanilla
   d) Carrot

295) Barney finds a briefcase containing how much money?
   a) $10,000
   b) $75,000
   c) $250,000
   d) $500,000

296) Andy works on a case with a blonde lawyer named:
   a) Lee Drake
   b) Betty Ann Quigley
   c) Tina Hopkins
   d) Becky Doyle

297) Aunt Bee wins a trip for two to where?
   a) Mexico
   b) Hollywood
   c) Paris
   d) Raleigh

292) Ernest T. Bass

293) Aunt Bee

294) Chocolate

295) $250,000

296) Lee Drake

297) Mexico

298) Opie gets fired from his job at:
   a) Weavers Department Store
   b) Feed and Grain
   c) Foley's Grocery Store
   d) Doakes' Market

299) What does Opie break while working at the drug store?
   a) A Lantern
   b) A Bottle
   c) A Broom
   d) The Cash Register

300) What do Barney and Mrs. Mendelbright enjoy doing on the front porch?
   a) Listening to hymn music
   b) Counting cars
   c) Looking at the stars
   d) Telling ghost stories

301) What is Andy's favorite kind of pie?
   a) Blueberry
   b) Gooseberry
   c) Apple
   d) Pecan

302) Who is a voice teacher?
   a) Gomer
   b) Glen Cripes
   c) Elenora Poultice
   d) Clara Edwards

303) Who is accused of drinking cooking sherry?
   a) Ernest T. Bass
   b) Malcolm Merriweather
   c) Briscoe Darling
   d) Aunt Bee

298) Doakes' Market

299) A Bottle

300) Counting cars

301) Gooseberry

302) Elenora Poultice

303) Malcolm Merriweather

304) Who "loses" his voice on the day of the chorale?
   a) Gomer
   b) Barney
   c) Andy
   d) Glen Cripes

305) Who does Goober NOT impersonate?
   a) William Holden
   b) Cary Grant
   c) Chester
   d) Edward G. Robinson

306) Who is seen smoking a cigarette from time to time?
   a) Floyd
   b) Howard
   c) Emmett
   d) Andy

307) Mrs. Mendelbright's life savings amounts to approximately how much?
   a) $1,000
   b) $3,600
   c) $5,400
   d) $8,700

308) What brand of car is the squad car?
   a) Ford
   b) Chevy
   c) Buick
   d) Chrysler

309) What group pastes current events in scrapbooks?
   a) Philomathian Literary Society
   b) The Contemporaries
   c) The Garden Club
   d) The Mayberry Library Club

304) Gomer

305) William Holden

306) Andy

307) $3,600

308) Ford

309) Philomathian Literary Society

310) Which of the following did Dud Wash NOT carry on his money belt while in the military?
   a) A hair ribbon
   b) Charlene's letters
   c) A rabbit's foot
   d) Flower petals

311) Who is a member of The Esquire Club?
   a) Roger Courtney
   b) Ben Johnson
   c) Barney Fife
   d) Clint Biggers

312) Who blackballed Howard Sprague?
   a) Floyd
   b) Goober
   c) Andy
   d) Emmett

313) Who, according to Barney, gets his jaw muscles workin' when he gets sore?
   a) Andy
   b) Ben Weaver
   c) Floyd
   d) Mr. Foley

314) What happens to Barney when he gets riled?
   a) He stomps his feet
   b) The vein in his neck sticks out
   c) He starts to sweat
   d) He loses his voice

310) A rabbit's foot

311) Roger Courtney

312) Goober

313) Andy

314) The vein in his neck sticks out

315) Who serves Andy and Opie a candlelight dinner?
   a) Peggy McMillan
   b) Helen Crump
   c) Aunt Bee
   d) Ellie Walker

316) What part does Andy play in the Centennial play?
   a) Tim C. Doyle
   b) Noogatuck
   c) James Merriweather
   d) John Mayberry

317) Who tells his brother he is a Deputy Sheriff?
   a) Otis
   b) Goober
   c) Gomer
   d) Howard

318) How many flying lessons does Aunt Bee take before she flies solo?
   a) 9
   b) 11
   c) 13
   d) 16

319) Who sang "Flow Gently, Sweet Afton"?
   a) Juanita Pike
   b) Juanita Beasley
   c) Aunt Bee
   d) Clara Edwards

320) Who is the shy lady that Barney walked to church on Sundays?
   a) Mrs. Mendelbright
   b) Miss Rosemary
   c) Miss Jane

315) Peggy McMillan

316) James Merriweather

317) Otis

318) 11

319) Juanita Pike

320) Miss Rosemary

321) What is the deluxe special at Morelli's Restaurant?
   a) Sea bass
   b) Chopped liver
   c) Pounded steak
   d) Lobster

322) What is Goober's record time for dismantling a carburetor?
   a) 15 min. & 102 sec.
   b) 27 min. & 12 sec.
   c) 38 min. & 12 sec.
   d) 47 min. & 12 sec.

323) How much does Barney weigh on his fifth anniversary as a Deputy Sheriff?
   a) 130 lbs.
   b) 138 lbs.
   c) 145 lbs.
   d) 149 lbs.

324) Who describes Aunt Bee's pickles as "kerosene cucumbers"?
   a) Andy
   b) Barney
   c) Clara Edwards
   d) Howard

325) Who studied at Bradberry Business College?
   a) Howard
   b) Emmett
   c) Floyd
   d) Goober

321) Pounded steak

322) 38 min. & 12 sec.

323) 138 lbs.

324) Barney

325) Howard

326) What was Barney cooking in his room when he was evicted by Mrs. Medelbright?
   a) Hamburgers
   b) Stew
   c) Chili
   d) Ravioli

327) Who is the star witness in the case of the punch in the nose?
   a) Floyd
   b) Goober
   c) Otis
   d) Opie

328) Who is NOT considered a good singer?
   a) Rafe Hollister
   b) Barney
   c) Charlene Darling
   d) Gomer

329) What musical instrument does Barney NOT play?
   a) Tambourine
   b) Cymbals
   c) Bongo Drums
   d) Harmonica

330) How many pancakes does Goober eat to win the County Fair contest?
   a) 22
   b) 32
   c) 45
   d) 57

326) Chili

327) Floyd

328) Barney

329) Tambourine

330) 57

331) At the County Fair shooting gallery, how many shots do you get for 25 cents?
   a) One
   b) Three
   c) Five
   d) Ten

332) Whose car does Goober assemble in the courthouse?
   a) Floyd's
   b) Gilly Walker's
   c) Malcolm Tucker's
   d) Barney's

333) Who "talks" to a hawk at the duck pond?
   a) Andy
   b) Barney
   c) Malcolm Merriweather
   d) Ernest T. Bass

334) Who sells his gas station to Ed Sawyer?
   a) Wally
   b) Goober
   c) David Browning
   d) George Sapperly

335) Who has red hair?
   a) Barney
   b) Opie
   c) Howard
   d) Gomer

331) Five

332) Gilly Walker's

333) Andy

334) George Sapperly

335) Opie

336) How much money does Aunt Bee win in Goober's "Grab Bag For Cash" contest?
- a) $1.00
- b) $3.00
- c) $5.00
- d) $10.00

337) Andy tries to pass Ernest T. Bass off as what person to Mrs. Wiley?
- a) Oliver Gossage
- b) Henry Wheeler
- c) Orville Hendricks
- d) Allan Newsome

338) What movie does Barney see the night before he tries to teach the bank a lesson?
- a) Hold-Up
- b) G-Men
- c) Kansas City Heist
- d) The Legend of Dillinger

339) Who is one of Daphne's boyfriends?
- a) Bill
- b) Al
- c) Scott
- d) Herb

340) Who wrote "Pickups and Splashes from Floor and Pool"?
- a) Andy
- b) Opie
- c) Barney
- d) Aunt Bee

336) $5.00

337) Oliver Gossage

338) G-Men

339) Al

340) Barney

341) How many wild birds does Opie raise after they lose their mother?
   a) 2
   b) 3
   c) 4
   d) 5

342) How many times does Barney capture Eddie Brooke?
   a) 1
   b) 2
   c) 3
   d) 4

343) Who is the "Merry Madcap of Mayberry"?
   a) Barney
   b) Howard
   c) Goober
   d) Emmett

344) Who is president of the Sheriff's Association?
   a) Sheriff Jackson
   b) Sheriff Patterson
   c) Sheriff Jones
   d) Sheriff Dillon

341) 3

342) 2

343) Howard Sprague

344) Sheriff Jackson

345) Which food item do Opie and his merry men NOT bring to Weary Willie?
   a) A Ham
   b) Blueberry pie
   c) Half a turkey
   d) Fresh vegetables

346) From the street, the courthouse door on the left has a sign that reads....
   a) Sheriff
   b) Justice of the Peace
   c) Welcome
   d) Mayberry Courthouse

347) Who practiced handcuff slapping on Barney?
   a) Opie
   b) Leon
   c) Gomer
   d) Goober

348) Who is Opie jealous of when Andy pays too much attention to him?
   a) Barney
   b) Tray
   c) Howie
   d) George Foley

349) What does Andy give Opie for supposedly earning straight A's?
   a) A chemistry set
   b) An erector set
   c) A new baseball glove
   d) A bicycle

345) Blueberry pie

346) Sheriff

347) Gomer

348) Tray

349) A bicycle

350) Which branch of the military does Ernest T. Bass try to join?
    a) Army
    b) Navy
    c) Marines
    d) Air Force

351) Which of the following does Ernest T. Bass NOT desire?
    a) A car
    b) A woman
    c) A uniform
    d) An education

352) What spoiled kid teaches Opie to throw temper tantrums?
    a) Whitey
    b) Arnold Winkler
    c) Howie Pruitt
    d) Arnold Bailey

353) Who sits in for Opie to practice the piano while Opie goes to football practice?
    a) Arnold Bailey
    b) Howie Pruitt
    c) Arnold Winkler
    d) George Foley

354) Who talks to his chickens like they are real people?
    a) Mr. Bristol
    b) Mr. Hendricks
    c) Sam Jones
    d) Fletch Dilbeck

355) Who sideswipes Ron Bailey's car?
    a) Goober
    b) Fletch
    c) Jud
    d) Rafe

350) Army

351) A car

352) Arnold Winkler

353) Arnold Bailey

354) Mr. Bristol

355) Fletch

356) Helen works on the grading manual with a handsome man named:
   a) Don
   b) James
   c) Frank
   d) Ron

357) Andy is jealous of Peggy's friend named:
   a) Peter
   b) Luther
   c) Clovis
   d) Don

358) Who is the leader of the convicts-at-large?
   a) Sally
   b) Naomi
   c) Maude
   d) Bertha

359) Who does Andy frighten away by asking him to go on a manhunt?
   a) Barney
   b) Ollie
   c) Howard
   d) Otis

360) What is the color of the horse Barney rides to save Andy from marriage?
   a) Black
   b) Brown
   c) Gray
   d) White

356) Frank

357) Don

358) Maude

359) Ollie

360) White

361) Which song is good old 14- A?
   a) "Leaning on the everlasting arms"
   b) "Welcome sweet springtime"
   c) "My hometown"
   d) "There is a time"

362) What is the cost for four ounces of Blue Moonlight perfume?
   a) $ 6.50
   b) $17.75
   c) $64.00
   d) $75.00

363) Whose business has a sign that reads, "We Don't Loan Tools"?
   a) Emmett's Fix-It Shop
   b) Wally's Service Station
   c) Monroe's Funeral Parlor
   d) Weaver's Department Store

364) What is Ellen Brown's chosen profession?
   a) Waitress
   b) Saleslady
   c) Wrestler
   d) Manicurist

365) What does Barney have on his person to help him pass his physical?
   a) A paper weight
   b) A gold bar
   c) A pocket full of quarters
   d) A dog tag and chain

361) "Welcome sweet springtime"

362) $64.00

363) Emmett's Fix-It Shop

364) Manicurist

365) A dog tag and chain

366) Who tries to con Barney into marrying her?
   a) Melissa Stevens
   b) Thelma Lou
   c) Ellie Walker
   d) Lydia Croswaith

367) Who do Opie's friends think is hanging himself in the Taylor's closet?
   a) Goober
   b) Old Man Remshaw
   c) Asa Breesey
   d) Barney

368) According to Goober, where is the finest trout fishing in the county?
   a) Myers Lake
   b) Lake Monroe
   c) Hopkins Lake
   d) Lake Maxinhall

369) Who sings "Texarkana in the morning"?
   a) Jim Lindsey
   b) Keevey Hazelton
   c) Rafe Hollister
   d) Rip Wilson

370) Who owns the book, "Jokes For All Occasions"?
   a) Opie
   b) Barney
   c) Howard
   d) Malcolm Merriweather

366) Melissa Stevens

367) Barney

368) Hopkins Lake

369) Keevey Hazelton

370) Howard

371) Who recites, "A Fading Flower of Forgotten Love"?
  a) Aunt Bee
  b) Clara Edwards
  c) John Masters
  d) Josephine Pike

372) How does Ernest T. Bass make up for being mean?
  a) By being smart
  b) By being real healthy
  c) By being good looking
  d) By being strong

373) What are the first names of the "fighting" Boone couple?
  a) Ed and Hazel
  b) Wilbert and Emma
  c) Fred and Jenny
  d) Sam and Glenda

374) In what city is TV station WZAZ located?
  a) Raleigh
  b) Greensboro
  c) Charlotte
  d) Siler City

375) Where can one find a poodle trimmer?
  a) Mt. Pilot
  b) Asheville
  c) Mt. Airy
  d) Durham

376) Opie and which friend find a baby on the courthouse step?
  a) Howie
  b) Arnold
  c) Tray
  d) Johnny Paul

371) Aunt Bee

372) By being real healthy

373) Fred and Jenny

374) Siler City

375) Mt. Pilot

376) Arnold

377) What gift does Opie purchase for his "crush", Miss Crump?
   a) Candy
   b) Jewelry
   c) Stockings
   d) A hat

378) Who raised Andy when he was a child?
   a) Rose
   b) Aunt Bee
   c) His grandmother
   d) Mrs. Wiley

379) What beverage does Barney drink that contains "knock out drops"?
   a) Milk
   b) Pop
   c) Water
   d) Beer

380) Who gives out fourteen traffic tickets in one day?
   a) Warren
   b) Goober
   c) Andy
   d) Barney

381) Name the female reporter who writes an undercover story on Andy.
   a) Jean Boswell
   b) Kate Jennings
   c) Melissa Stevens
   d) Becky Doyle

377) Stockings

378) Aunt Bee

379) Milk

380) Goober

381) Jean Boswell

382) What day is Walker's Drug Store closed during a non-holiday week?
   a) Sunday
   b) Wednesday
   c) Friday
   d) None of the above

383) What is Millie's last name?
   a) Jones
   b) Perkins
   c) Hopkins
   d) Hutchins

384) Which girl does Barney NOT send to Andy's house as a prospective date?
   a) Amanda
   b) Rosemary
   c) Mary
   d) Blanche

385) Which Darling family son plays the mandolin?
   a) Dean
   b) Rodney
   c) Mitch
   d) Doug

386) Who is the town mortician?
   a) Orville Hendricks
   b) Orville Monroe
   c) Jimmy Janson
   d) Doc Harvey

382) None of the above

383) Hutchins

384) Mary

385) Dean

386) Orville Monroe

387) What does the bully charge Opie for passing by his street?
   a) 1 cent
   b) 5 cents
   c) 10 cents
   d) 25 cents

388) What does Hilda Mae call Barney to get him to vote for Ellie Walker?
   a) Handsome
   b) Suave
   c) Honey Pie
   d) Cream Puff

389) What actor portrayed the voice of Leonard Blush?
   a) George Lindsey
   b) Don Knotts
   c) Howard Morris
   d) Ken Berry

390) Otis creates a mosaic design of what animal?
   a) Cow
   b) Horse
   c) Dog
   d) Sheep

391) Who is noted for having lots of magazines in his place of business?
   a) Howard
   b) Emmett
   c) Floyd
   d) Goober

387) 5 cents

388) Cream Puff

389) Howard Morris

390) Cow

391) Floyd

392) Who does Otis sell his car to?
   a) Aunt Bee
   b) Goober
   c) Luke Jensen
   d) Charlie Varney

393) What vision issue does Luke Jensen have?
   a) Nearsighted
   b) Farsighted
   c) Astigmatism
   d) Blind in one eye

394) To make Barney jealous, Thelma Lou goes on a date with whom?
   a) Goober
   b) Howard
   c) Gomer
   d) Andy

395) What is the name of Opie's next door neighbor?
   a) Judy
   b) Heather
   c) Gloria
   d) Sally

396) What does Goober forget to order after taking over the gas station?
   a) Wiper blades
   b) Oil
   c) Pop
   d) Gas

392) Charlie Varney

393) Nearsighted

394) Gomer

395) Heather

396) Gas

397) Who wins the turkey shoot 2 years in a row?
   a) Goober
   b) Andy
   c) Fletch
   d) Barney

398) How does Floyd describe Neil Bentley?
   a) A nice man
   b) A sharp dresser
   c) A crook
   d) A swindler

399) What is the cost for single room with no bath at The Mayberry Hotel?
   a) $1.00/night
   b) $1.75/night
   c) $2.50/night
   d) $2.75/night

400) How far is Raleigh from Mayberry?
   a) 12 miles
   b) 22 miles
   c) 35 miles
   d) 55 miles

401) Which barbershop quartet member gets laryngitis?
   a) Gomer
   b) Andy
   c) Howard
   d) Skippy

402) How much is a flat top at Floyd's?
   a) 75 cents
   b) $1.00
   c) $1.75
   d) $2.00

397) Goober

398) A nice man

399) $1.75/night

400) 55 miles

401) Howard

402) $2.00

403) Who gives Barney a nickel with the buffalo "pointing the wrong way"?
   a) Andy
   b) Ellie
   c) Otis
   d) Floyd

404) What does Gomer wear for his first military inspection?
   a) His khaki's
   b) Sgt. Carter's dress blues
   c) Bib overalls
   d) Jeans

405) What is Warren's relation to Floyd?
   a) Nephew
   b) Cousin
   c) Son
   d) Grandson

406) How much will spark plugs cost Mr. Tucker?
   a) 75 cents /each
   b) 85 cents /each
   c) $1.00 / each
   d) $1.15 / each

407) How much money does Floyd "apparently" win in Goober's "cash giveaway"?
   a) $25
   b) $100
   c) $200
   d) $500

403) Andy

404) Sgt. Carter's dress blues

405) Nephew

406) $1.15 / each

407) $200

408) Who does Barney say has "hot knees"?
   a) Thelma Lou
   b) Helen
   c) Andy
   d) Lydia

409) What was Barney's nickname in high school?
   a) Squeaky
   b) Rifle Fife
   c) Fast gun Fife
   d) Slim

410) How much does Gomer pay for his black dress shoes for his date with Mary Grace?
   a) $5
   b) $8
   c) $10
   d) $13.75

411) What "magic word" makes a gumball machine dispense free gumballs?
   a) Shazam
   b) Bingo
   c) Alacazam
   d) Tuscarora

412) Who is Goobers first date?
   a) Lydia
   b) Flora
   c) Helen
   d) Judith

408) Andy

409) Rifle Fife

410) $8

411) Tuscarora

412) Lydia

413) Whose father owns the R&M Grain Elevators?
   a) Helen Crump
   b) Peggy McMillan
   c) Thelma Lou
   d) Alice Von Drusek

414) What does Barney's cousin Virgil give to Opie?
   a) $5.00
   b) Wood carvings
   c) A lucky nickel
   d) A painting

415) What does Opie NOT wish for from The Count?
   a) A jackknife
   b) A "B" in arithmetic
   c) Helen as his 6th grade teacher
   d) Andy and Helen to get married

416) What business does Andy run as a side business?
   a) Laundromat
   b) Butchers
   c) Car dealership
   d) Printers

417) In what city was Helen Crump arrested?
   a) Cincinnati
   b) Kansas City
   c) Indianapolis
   d) Detroit

413) Peggy McMillan

414) Wood carvings

415) Andy and Helen to get married

416) Laundromat

417) Kansas City

418) Who breaks a date with Opie to go out with a popular boy in school?
   a) Mary Wiggins
   b) Karen Folker
   c) Haley Hopkins
   d) Mary Alice Carter

419) Whom does Opie try and sell his bike to?
   a) Whitey
   b) Howie
   c) Arnold
   d) Tray

420) Who catches seven perch and six largemouth bass in one weekend?
   a) Goober
   b) Howard
   c) Andy
   d) Opie

421) Who puts Otis to hard labor?
   a) Barney
   b) Warren
   c) Helen
   d) Aunt Bee

422) Why does Andy say he lost to Helen in bowling?
   a) Bad back
   b) Head cold
   c) Rented shoes
   d) Pants too tight

418) Mary Alice Carter

419) Howie

420) Goober

421) Aunt Bee

422) Rented shoes

423) What is the name of the Hollywood producer looking to make a movie in Mayberry?
  a) Mr. Harmon
  b) Mr. Smith
  c) Mr. Johnson
  d) Mr. Petersen

424) Who does Otis mistake for the "loaded goat"?
  a) Aunt Bessie
  b) Uncle Nat
  c) Cousin Egbert
  d) Grandpa Pyle

425) What is Goober's least favorite season?
  a) Spring
  b) Summer
  c) Fall
  d) Winter

426) Who drives Andy and Helen to the Myers Lake picnic?
  a) Barney
  b) Goober
  c) Howard
  d) Gomer

427) How much does a temporary deputy earn for a day's service?
  a) $2.00
  b) $5.00
  c) $10.00
  d) $15.00

423) Mr. Harmon

424) Uncle Nat

425) Winter

426) Goober

427) $5.00

428) Who sings "No count Mule"
   a) Andy
   b) Barney
   c) Gomer
   d) Otis

429) Who has an uncle named Edward?
   a) Helen
   b) Thelma Lou
   c) Aunt Bee
   d) Floyd

430) What is Mrs. Lesch's first name?
   a) Myrt
   b) Edna
   c) Emma
   d) Gertrude

431) Who sings "Eatin' Goober Peas"?
   a) Ernest T. Bass
   b) Otis
   c) Floyd
   d) Nobody

432) Charlene offers what dish to Andy and Barney for dinner?
   a) Possum
   b) Roots and berries
   c) Fish muddle
   d) Crow

433) Who brings his "Wild West" show to Mayberry?
   a) Fred Gibson
   b) George Wilson
   c) Jed Thurston
   d) Mel Blanc

428) Gomer

429) Helen

430) Myrt

431) Nobody

432) Fish muddle

433) Fred Gibson

434) What year was "The Andy Griffith Show" first shown on television?
   a) 1959
   b) 1960
   c) 1961
   d) 1963

435) Barney says he is not superstitious, he is just..... ?
   a) Cautious
   b) Conservative
   c) Afraid
   d) Suspicious

436) Floyd informs Andy that the dingo dog is indigenous to what country?
   a) China
   b) Mexico
   c) Russia
   d) Australia

437) Where can the fish "Old Sam" be found?
   a) Myers Lake
   b) Hopkins Lake
   c) Tucker's Lake
   d) Culver's Lake

438) What item is Cousin Virgil able to open?
   a) Desk drawer
   b) Bank vault
   c) Cell door
   d) Courthouse door

434) 1960

435) Cautious

436) Australia

437) Tucker's Lake

438) Cell door

439) What is the name of the flying school Aunt Bee attended?
a) MacDonald's
b) Johnson's
c) A-1 Flying
d) Earhart's

440) What is the maximum wattage light bulb allowed in one of Mrs. Mendelbright's rooms for rent?
a) 40
b) 50
c) 75
d) 100

441) Name Malcolm Merriweather's hometown.
a) Leeds
b) Dewsbury
c) Heckmondwike
d) Liversedge

442) How many "Claudes" are in the Beamon family?
a) 1
b) 2
c) 3
d) 4

443) Who was a Mayor of Mayberry?
a) Smith
b) Jenkins
c) Montgomery
d) Newdale

444) Who used to sip all the syrup from Barney's snow cones?
a) Viki Harms
b) Maya Lambert
c) Joyce Wilson
d) Lily Hopkins

439) MacDonald's

440) 40

441) Heckmondwike

442) 3

443) Jenkins

444) Viki Harms

445) Who replaces Barney as soloist for the song Santa Lucia?
   a) Andy
   b) Gomer
   c) Goober
   d) Rafe

446) What song does Opie sing for the Darling's?
   a) "There is a time"
   b) "Dooley"
   c) "You get a line"
   d) "Ol' Dan Tucker"

447) What item does Otis drink out of while "serving out his sentence" at the Taylor house?
   a) A Vase
   b) A Shoe
   c) A Pitcher
   d) A Bowl

448) Who was able to hit the bell 8 consecutive times at the County Fair?
   a) Ernest T. Bass
   b) Gomer
   c) Opie
   d) Goober

449) What day of the week does Goober dismantle Gilly's car?
   Monday
   a) Tuesday
   b) Wednesday
   c) Thursday

445) Gomer

446) "Ol' Dan Tucker"

447) A Vase

448) Goober

449) Wednesday

450) Who does Ernest T. Bass have tutor him?
    a) Andy
    b) Barney
    c) Aunt Bee
    d) Opie

451) Name the saxophone player who is hard of hearing.
    a) Jud
    b) Melvin
    c) Luther
    d) Ray

452) Why does Rose Pine leave her job with the Taylors?
    a) To get married
    b) She is being deported
    c) She gets another job
    d) Andy fires her

453) Johnny Paul wins a baseball bat at the :
    a) Shooting gallery
    b) Dunking booth
    c) Ring toss
    d) Putt putt

454) What Mayberrian played professional football?
    a) Dick Brutus
    b) Flip Conroy
    c) Flash Nelson
    d) Herman Glimpshire

455) What do the men of Mayberry think Wilbur Finch does for a living?
    a) Shoe salesman
    b) Movie star
    c) Record producer
    d) Talent scout

450) Andy

451) Luther

452) To get married

453) Ring toss

454) Flip Conroy

455) Talent scout

456) Why does Andy lock up Sam Muggins?
   a) Stealing
   b) Behind on his bills
   c) Moonshining
   d) Public intoxication

457) Who sings "Away in a Manger"?
   a) Ellie Walker
   b) Aunt Bee
   c) Peggy McMillan
   d) Clara Edwards

458) Who thought Andy made a marriage proposal to her?
   a) Helen
   b) Mary
   c) Ellen
   d) Sharon

459) Who turns down Andy's marriage proposal?
   a) Helen
   b) Thelma Lou
   c) Mary
   d) Ellie

460) What does Opie teach Helen Crump's niece to do?
   a) Hoola-hoop
   b) Roller Skate
   c) Ice Skate
   d) Juggle

461) Who is considering buying Gilly Walker's car?
   a) Floyd
   b) Otis
   c) Barney
   d) Goober

456) Moonshining

457) Ellie Walker

458) Ellen

459) Ellie Walker

460) Roller Skate

461) Floyd

462) The yearly budget for Emmet's Fix-It Shop is..?
    a) Zero
    b) $24
    c) $100
    d) $175

463) What starlet does Andy go out with in Hollywood?
    a) Darlene Mason
    b) Geraldine Hammons
    c) Bernadette Crosby
    d) Angela Lomax

464) What is named "Deep Pink Ecstasy"?
    a) A rose
    b) A dog
    c) A perfume
    d) A car

465) Who spends a birthday in jail?
    a) Sam Muggins
    b) Mr. Weaver
    c) Dan Caldwell
    d) Otis

466) Sam Jones has a son named:
    a) Steve
    b) Clovis
    c) Mike
    d) Jimmy

467) What item was Jim Lindsey going to leave behind to cover his bills?
    a) A gold coin
    b) A watch
    c) An autographed picture
    d) A guitar

462) $24

463) Darlene Mason

464) A rose

465) Otis

466) Mike

467) A watch

468) What is the make of car that Barney buys from the "little old lady from Mount Pilot"?
   a) Ford
   b) Chevy
   c) Oldsmobile
   d) Dodge

469) Which was NOT one of Barney's high school activities?
   a) Hall Monitor
   b) Tin Foil Drive
   c) Spanish Club
   d) Basketball

470) How does Opie address his dad?
   a) Pops
   b) Daddy
   c) Pa
   d) Old man

471) What does the shoe salesman try unsuccessfully to rent in Mayberry?
   a) A car
   b) A TV
   c) A bus
   d) A cot

472) What type of shot does nurse Mary Simpson give to Rafe Hollister?
   a) Tetanus
   b) Hepatitis
   c) Chicken pox
   d) Flu

468) Ford

469) Basketball

470) Pa

471) A TV

472) Tetanus

473) Who replaced Ernest T. Bass at the school crossing?
   a) Goober
   b) Malcolm
   c) Barney
   d) Andy

474) Which sheriff, according to Andy, had a "fat and stupid" deputy?
   a) Sheriff Jackson
   b) Matt Dillon
   c) Buford T. Justice
   d) Sheriff of Nottingham

475) Opie was saving his money to buy a coat for whom?
   a) Sharon
   b) Charlotte
   c) Mary
   d) Jenny

476) Andy buys Aunt Bee a new:
   a) TV
   b) Car
   c) Freezer
   d) Phonograph

477) What is Andy's middle name?
   e) Jackson
   f) Paul
   g) Samuel
   h) Edward

478) What are the jail visiting hours?
   a) 24 hours
   b) 2 p.m. – 4 p.m.
   c) 3 p.m. – 6 p.m.
   d) 6 p.m. – 8 p.m.

473) Malcolm

474) Sheriff of Nottingham

475) Charlotte

476) Freezer

477) Jackson

478) 2 p.m. – 4 p.m.

479) What color socks does Gomer wear for his date with Mary Grace?
- a) Black
- b) White
- c) Yellow
- d) Purple

480) What is the name of the horse Opie is hired to feed?
- a) Jenny
- b) Trigger
- c) Dolly
- d) Trixie

481) Who runs against Sam Jones for head of City Council?
- a) Emmett
- b) Barney
- c) Andy
- d) Goober

482) Name one thing NOT wrong with the Taylor house
- a) Noisy pipes
- b) Squeaking floors
- c) Crack in ceiling
- d) Roof leaks

483) Who was Mayberry's first Indian agent?
- a) Seth Taylor
- b) Lucious Pyle
- c) Daniel Lawson
- d) Gale Edwards

484) Who is a stone mason in Mayberry?
- a) Brian Jackson
- b) Biff Henderson
- c) Clyde Mason
- d) Jimmy Jackson

479) Yellow

480) Dolly

481) Emmett

482) Squeaking floors

483) Daniel Lawson

484) Brian Jackson

485) Which Taylor relative has a statue made of his likeness?
   a) Seth Taylor
   b) Jackson Taylor
   c) Wendell Taylor
   d) Harold Taylor

486) What is the last name of the boy, from a wealthy family, that Opie meets at camp?
   a) Tarkington
   b) Hollander
   c) Pruitt
   d) Herzog

487) What type of trees does Aunt Bee want to plant on Elm Street?
   a) Magnolia
   b) Birch
   c) Elm
   d) Buckeye

488) What color are the courthouse walls?
   a) Blue
   b) Green
   c) Brown
   d) White

489) How many dogs does Barney take out to the field to run around?
   a) 3
   b) 7
   c) 9
   d) 11

485) Seth Taylor

486) Hollander

487) Magnolia

488) Green

489) 11

490) What is Aunt Bee's slogan when running for City Council?
   a) Beautify Mayberry
   b) The will of the people
   c) A flower in every pot
   d) It's not pot luck

491) Whom does Ben Weaver want to evict for not paying the rent?
   a) Frank Myers
   b) Lester Scoby
   c) Otis Campbell
   d) Luke Jensen

492) Whose death comes as a terrible blow to Aunt Bee?
   a) Millie Goss'
   b) Jenny Parmenter's
   c) Wilford Hannover's
   d) Augusta Finch's

493) In what Northeastern city does Madeline Grayson say she owns a home?
   a) Baltimore
   b) Boston
   c) Bangor
   d) Washington, DC

494) At what time of the day does Augusta Finch pass away?
   a) 5 a.m.
   b) 10:30 am
   c) 6 p.m.
   d) Midnight

490) The will of the people

491) Lester Scoby

492) Augusta Finch's

493) Baltimore

494) 10:30 A. M.

495) What does Floyd say "Tempus Edax Rerum" means?
    a) Time heals everything
    b) You can't look back
    c) Hindsight is 20/20
    d) The weather sure is funny

496) Who was never in the real estate business?
    a) Mr. Schlummer
    b) Barney
    c) Floyd
    d) Tom Biggers

497) Where does Goober take his old friend Roy Swanson to dinner?
    a) Moreli's
    b) The Golden Palace
    c) The Burger Barn
    d) Aunt Bee's Canton Palace

498) Who was NOT a doctor in Mayberry?
    a) Doc Winters
    b) Doc Carruthers
    c) Doc Robbins
    d) Doc Harvey

499) Who threw a no-hitter against Mt. Pilot?
    a) Andy
    b) Barney
    c) Goober
    d) Emmett

500) Who won first prize in the pansy division at the Garden Club show?
    a) Howard
    b) Floyd
    c) Andy
    d) Aunt Bee

495) Time heals everything

496) Floyd

497) The Golden Palace

498) Doc Robbins

499) Andy

500) Floyd

TRUE OR FALSE

1) The cave Andy and Helen become "trapped" in is called Lost Lovers' Cave.

2) Andy says he has never been without clean underwear while on a trip, thanks to Aunt Bee.

3) Gomer wants a tattoo put on his arm before he joins the Marines.

4) Mr. Dave's magic fishing lure is called the Gollysplasher.

5) Barney knows an old German soldier.

6) According to Barney, everything a Fife eats turns to energy.

7) Barney's father never hit him.

8) Ernest T. Bass hit Charlene Darling in the head with a rock.

9) Emma Watson regularly takes pills that cost 10 cents.

10) Aunt Bee once portrayed Madame Curie in a Sunday School class play.

11) Ramona Wiley's married name is Bektoris.

12) Colonel Harvey describes the Indians he lived among as sinners.

1) True

2) False (A brown paper sack full of sandwiches)

3) True (An eagle with the word "Mother")

4) False (Gollywobbler)

5) True (Hugo Hopfleish)

6) False (it turns to muscle)

7) True (Barney was bigger than he was)

8) False (he hit Hogette Winslow)

9) True

10) False (she played the queen)

11) True

12) False (they're devils)

13) Ramona Wiley thinks Barney is a bartender.

14) According to Daphne, Raleigh has a club with a floor show.

15) Barney says the Tip Top Café might be serving liquor.

16) Andy gets a sprained wrist from fighting Daphne's boyfriend.

17) Barney unsuccessfully leads a group of women in singing "Row, Row, Row Your Boat."

18) Mrs. Heidelbright was known as the "Beast of the Fourth Floor."

19) According to Mountain Folklore, if you sleep on a willow chip that has been under a sleeping dog's head you will have the same dream the dog had.

20) Andy told Reverend Tucker that the reason Barney was nodding off in church was because he had been up with Otis all night.

21) One of Frank Myers' ancestors once shook hands with General Robert E. Lee.

22) According to Barney, Frank Sinatra's music should be played after an intimate dinner.

23) Goober, Judd, and Otis are to be notified by mail if they are chosen to be deputies.

13) True

14) False (Yahtzee)

15) True

16) False (a black eye)

17) True

18) False (Mrs. Von Roeder)

19) 19. True

20) False (Andy had him on a chicken stakeout until 4 a.m.)

21) True

22) False (Cole Porter)

23) True

24) Goober, Judd and Otis receive free movie passes as compensation for their roles as deputies.

25) According to Barney, jaywalking is rampant in Mayberry.

26) Barney wears his uniform when he hitchhikes.

27) Malcolm Tucker's car is a six cylinder.

28) Barney has to stake out Al's Poultry Headquarters.

29) Mayberry's memorial horse trough is named after Seth Taylor.

30) Opie donated three cents to the underprivileged children's fund.

31) The Mayor's daughter is always the Mayberry Potato Queen.

32) The state traveling museum stops in Mayberry.

33) Biggs' Furniture pushes Ben Weaver into giving things away.

34) Barney gets upset when people say he is sensitive.

35) Daphne's boyfriend refers to Andy and Barney as "shrimps."

36) In a sermon, Dr. Breen asks Mayberrians, "What's your hurry?"

24) False ($5 Check)

25) True

26) True

27) False (Eight)

28) True

29) (False) David Mendelbright Memorial Horse Trough

30) True

31) False (several girls take turns)

32) True

33) False (Bert Miller's stand does)

34) True

35) False (Squirts)

36) True

37) Ernest T. Bass gets a gold tooth.

38) Madeline Grayson thinks Opie and Andy are brothers.

39) Daphne refers to Otis as a smelly old drunk.

40) Goober passes Barney's quick reflexes test at the Deputy Sheriff lineup.

41) Barney suggests Andy visit a "Swingers' " club at Miami Beach.

42) Barney needs a sugar pick-me-up late in the day.

43) Gomer does an impersonation of Edward G. Robinson.

44) Barney runs for Mayor of Mayberry.

45) The only thing that stands betwixt Ernest T. and sweet romance back in the hills is an education.

46) According to Barney, losing to a woman is the end of an era.

47) Aunt Bee says that, according to Andy, the Lord made two sexes: men and gossips.

48) In the good luck chant that begins, "Come fish, come," Sam is at the gate with a frosted cake.

37) False (It's just gold leaf done by a sign company)

38) True

39) False (Nice chubby drunk)

40) True

41) False ("Rabbit-Girl" club)

42) True

43) False (Goober does)

44) False

45) False (A uniform)

46) True

47) False (men and blabbermouths)

48) True

49) Nate Bracey, Andy and Barney's high school classmate, says he took speech lessons.

50) Emma Watson is a chronic jaywalker.

51) The Gordon Boys keep their moonshine still in Sleepy Hollow.

52) Buzz Fluhart studied the influence of atmospheric rays in relation to being a jinx.

53) Aunt Bee refers to Andy as a naked savage.

54) Someone wrote "Bobby Gribble hates Emma Larch" in the sidewalk in front of Floyd's.

55) From the street, the courthouse door on the left has the mail slot.

56) Gomer uses limburger cheese and a slice of onion for bait to catch a fish.

57) Barney uses a disguise from the Crime Fighters Weekly magazine to avoid being recognized as a peeping Tom.

58) Thelma Lou once bought lunch for Gomer.

59) The Taylors are the only people who are allowed to use Goober's tools.

60) Dud Wash "made eyes" at Idell Bushy.

49) False (dance lessons)

50) True

51) False (Franklin Hollow)

52) True

53) False (she calls Opie a naked savage)

54) True

55) False

56) True

57) False (A disguise from Opie's Jr. Detective Kit)

58) True

59) False (Only Goober's relatives)

60) True

61) According to Opie, a horse hair in your pocket will protect you in your travels.

62) Eventually, Thelma Lou marries Barney.

63) Rule # 2 at the Mayberry jail is "lights out at 8pm".

64) Nate Bushy's regular date to the town dance is his mother.

65) In Opie's dream about track and field day, the last event he wins is the pole vault.

66) Andy says Aunt Bee has a mean left jab and fancy footwork.

67) Some members of the Beamon family have a hooked nose.

68) Opie says Johnny Paul Jason is so wise because he reads in bed with a flashlight.

69) Barney's dog, Blue, dislikes lollipops.

70) Barney's uniform is made of genuine whiplash cord.

71) Gomer's dog was sweet but temperamental.

72) Barney says his paycheck should be made out to Barney fool.

73) Dixie Bell Edwards goes hunting in the Great Dismal Swamp.

61) False (A penny run over by a train)

62) True (in "Return to Mayberry")

63) False (No writing on the walls)

64) True

65) False (The ten-mile run)

66) True

67) False (they have an overbite)

68) True

69) False

70) True

71) False (sweet but dumb)

72) False (Barney Sucker)

73) True

74) Otis hit his wife with a leg of lamb.

75) Eagle Rock looks like an eagle.

76) Harvey Willick got a 2 cc injection of saline solution right in the medulla oblongata.

77) Ethel Page and her canary performed at the Pot o' Honey restaurant.

78) Gomer's parents "sealed the deal" on their marriage in writing.

79) Andy says kids in Norway have hardtack and raw fish for lunch.

80) Barney first introduces Andy to Lydia Crosswaith at the Tip Top Café.

81) The Morrison sisters view Panama Canal Day as a special holiday.

82) Barney says a man who keeps putting off marriage is happier.

83) Andy tells the Darlings he has witchery on his daddy's side.

84) The waitresses at the waffle house in Raleigh wear miniskirts.

85) Andy's uses a book as his weapon of choice in his fight with "Clarence Earp."

86) Frank Myers has a letter from President Grant.

74) False

75) True

76) False (Right in the gluteus maximus)

77) True

78) False (They shook hands)

79) True

80) 80. False (The fun girls)

81) True

82) False (He gets irritable)

83) False (his mama's side)

84) False (Peek-a-boo blouses)

85) True

86) False (Jefferson Davis)

87) The Snakeskin Creek got dammed up shortly before Andy went on a vacation.

88) The gold truck that passes through Mayberry is worth seven million dollars.

89) Don Knotts' favorite episode was "The Pickle Story.

90) Andy calls Barney's technique for probing the subconscious mind "The Barney Fife Mind Melder".

91) Andy calls Barney's sobriety test "The Barney Fife Peter Piper Nose-Pinching Test for Drunks."

92) Mrs. McGruder supposedly cannot clean the bank because she suffers from "the versitus."

93) Laura Lee Hobbs works at the dime store.

94) Opie's rock band is called The Mayberrites.

95) According to Barney a lot of people lie at lunch.

96) Howard Sprague helps paint Sam Jones' house.

97) The gold truck left the Denver Mint bound for Fort Knox.

98) Ben Sewell is protesting the gold truck shipment by carrying a sign.

87) True

88) False (It was a decoy)

89) True

90) False (Barney Fife Subconscious Prober Primer)

91) True

92) False (fungus of the knee)

93) True

94) False (The Sound Committee)

95) True

96) True

97) True

98) False (Regis carries the sign)

99) After she gets married, Rose's legal name is Rose Pine.

100) Dud gives Charlene a ruby ring.

101) Ellie Walker graduated from Bernard University.

102) Barney's cousin Virgil is from New York.

103) Andy once bought Opie a new car for his birthday.

104) Dick Renneker probably fears a sudden rainstorm

105) Rafe Hollister says he is "dang hot" when he has a fever.

106) The Morrison sisters turn in Big Jack Anderson for moonshining.

107) Frankie Flint is a farmhand.

108) Ellie wants to give Frankie Flint free health care products.

109) The Ladies' Aid Church Committee gets gassed on Colonel Harvey's Indian Elixir.

110) Don Knotts' hometown is Wheeling, West Virginia.

111) Parnell Rigsby lives in Siler City.

99) True

100) False (A tiger eye)

101) True

102) False (New Jersey)

103) False

104) False (sudden wind)

105) True

106) False (Ben Sewell and Rube Sloan)

107) True

108) False (makeup and perfume)

109) True

110) False (Morgantown, West Virginia)

111) False (Bannertown)

112) The breakfast special at the "Y" in Raleigh is served between 5 and 6 am.

113) Leonard Blush once sang the National Anthem at the county hog-calling contest.

114) Barney tells a busload of tourists he has been stuck with the name "Fast Gun Fife."

115) The Morrison sisters routinely tie up the phone for a good 3-4 hours on Sunday afternoon.

116) Bruce Flowers can only sing high after a fight with his mother.

117) According to Barney, if you are riding into the wind and put your tongue on the roof of your mouth, it is impossible to pronounce a word that begins with the letter S.

118) Francis Bavier (Aunt Bee) once lived in Morgantown, West Virginia.

119) Barney sends Helen Crump to Andy's house as a potential mate.

120) According to Ernest T. Bass, the name Hogette has a French origin.

121) The bookie barber tells Floyd he will work for minimum wage.

112) True

113) False (County Insecticide Convention)

114) True

115) False (Mendelbright Sisters)

116) True

117) True

118) True

119) False

120) True

121) False (commission)

122) Goober has seen the movie "The Monster that Ate Minnesota" ten times.

123) Andelina Darling Wash's dowry includes 16 chickens.

124) According to Barney, a wild pheasant is possibly the most difficult wild bird to ensnare.

125) Briscoe Darling got married when he was fourteen.

126) If you dip your hat in the horse trough, you have committed a 907.

127) Floyd charges tourists a dollar to see the Mayberry Jail.

128) Gomer tightens the on/off toggle on Andy's vacuum cleaner.

129) The Tip Top Café has a floor show.

130) Opie has a pet frog named Croak.

131) Jed Darling is the fun-loving one.

132) Barney buys a tin inkblot as a trick to play on Aunt Bee.

122) True

123) False

124) True

125) False (thirty)

126) True

127) False (2 bits apiece)

128) True

129) False (The Gigolo Club does)

130) False

131) False (Rodney)

132) True

133) Prior to using Miracle Salve, "Dr. Pendyke" had allegedly been using Miracle Mange Cure on his animals.

134) Jeff Pruitt picks up women on the street corner to check their weight.

135) The parking time limit on Main Street is two hours.

136) Nelvin puts up a quarantine sign to keep peddlers and agents away.

137) The song "There is a Time" makes Briscoe Darling cry.

138) The name Lydia means "Native of Lydia" in Ancient Greece.

139) Lydia Crosswaithe is from Greece.

140) According to the song, Aunt Maria jumped in the pot when the fire was too hot.

141) The Fife fellow who was related to Nathan Tibbs spelled his last name F-y-f-e.

142) Clark Cooper slits his shoes.

143) Aunt Bee writes "Amusing Tales for Tiny Tots".

144) John Masters is a hotel clerk.

145) According to Barney, things like love and good health make you rich.

133) False (Molly Harkin's Mange Cure)

134) True

135) False (One hour)

136) True

137) True

138) True

139) False (Greensboro)

140) True

141) False (Phyfe)

142) True

143) False (Helen Crump)

144) True

145) False (Love and Friendship)

146) Barney's nickname in judo class is "The Chicken".

147) Doc Andrews delivered Opie.

148) The book "Psychic Phenomena" was written by Dr. Merle Osmond.

149) Ernest T. Bass plans to buy a tent and a lantern for his honeymoon with his "Sweet Romeena."

150) Luke Comstock runs a chain of bicycle shops.

151) Luke Comstock lives in Cleveland.

152) The adult price of an issue of the Mayberry Sun is five cents.

153) Barney once arrested Mayor Stoner for vagrancy and loitering.

154) Wilbur Finch works for the North Carolina Shoe Company.

155) Andy once shot a man in the line of duty.

156) Aunt Bee and Clara Johnson attended Our Lady of Mayberry School together.

157) Barney had a column in his high school newspaper.

146) True

147) False (Dr. Bennett)

148) True

149) True

150) False (a chain of TV repair shops)

151) True

152) False (3 cents)

153) False (Mayor Pike)

154) False (Manhattan Shoe Company)

155) True (Luke Comstock, in the leg)

156) False (Sweetbriar Normal School)

157) True

158) Lester Scobey finally gets a job at the bank.

159) Opie and his friends hope to win a bicycle by selling Miracle Salve.

160) Fred Goss suggests Opie buy a blue suit to save himself some trouble.

161) Briscoe Darling's high water mark for pie is three cuts.

162) Andy briefly considers moving to South America.

163) T. Jonathon Osgood wrote "Poems of Romance".

164) J. Howard Jackson is an attorney.

165) According to Barney, all of God's children have a uvula.

166) Barney likes sourdough bread for his sandwiches.

167) Hazel plays the piano on good ol'14- A.

168) Andy says he always likes to do at least 50 push-ups each day.

169) Opie had a dog named Gulliver.

170) The deluxe special at Morrelli's is $2.99.

158) False (Weaver's department store)

159) False (a pony)

160) False (Whiskey colored)

161) True

162) True

163) True

164) False (Publisher)

165) True

166) False (Salt-rising bread)

167) True

168) False (15)

169) True

170) False ($1.85)

171) The "convicts at large" claim to be with Girl Campers of America.

172) The Wakefields are feuding with the McCoys.

173) Andy Griffith grew up on the corner of Rockford and Haymore streets.

174) Barney, "the lady gambler", has to go behind the barn to take a pinch of snuff.

175) Mrs. Mendelbright got the dresser in Barney's room from her mother.

176) "Enquiring Minds" magazine focuses on a new subject each month.

177) Otis was first booked for intoxication on Sept 23, 1941.

178) According to Barney, bird eggs can make you go crazy if they get in your hair.

179) Barney wants to send his motorcycle to the Smith Brothers Institution in Washington, D.C.

180) Andy gives "how to be nice" lessons to the Mr. and Mrs. Scobey.

181) Henry Wheeler asks to borrow an onion from Aunt Bee for his stew.

171) True

172) False (Carters)

173) True

174) False (To the gas station)

175) True

176) False (Learn-a-Month magazine)

177) True

178) False (Bat or moth eggs)

179) True

180) False (The Boones)

181) True

182) The song "Dooley" makes Charlene Darling cry.

183) According to Barney and his voice teacher, a choir without a tenor is like a star without its glimmer.

184) According to Barney, Super Vac is the #1 vacuum cleaner in America.

185) Barney needs to eat lunch by noon or he'll get a headache.

186) Aunt Bee was the best dribbler on the Sweetbriar Normal School Women's basketball team.

187) Mayberry was founded by John Mayberry.

188) "Dooley" is a song that makes Briscoe Darling cry.

189) Howard Sprague performs bird calls on Colonel Tim's Talent Time.

190) Weary Willie, the hobo, says he has a fracture of the Femoral Lante

191) Prior to the construction of the new highway, emergency vehicles had to travel around Fisher's Pond.

192) On Friday nights, the special at the diner is pounded steak.

193) According to Barney, one sermon topic that you can't talk enough about is sin.

182) False

183) True

184) False (Miracle Sweep Vacuum)

185) True

186) False (Clara Johnson)

187) True

188) False

189) False

190) False (Fracture of the Petulla Oblongata)

191) True

192) False (Catfish casserole)

193) True

194) Gomer buys copper tubing at an auction.

195) Elizabeth Crowley, the "woman speeder," was driving 70 mph when Andy and Barney saw her speeding.

196) Briscoe Darling's wife's first husband was killed by a rattlesnake.

197) The Taylor's attend The All Souls Church.

198) Andy has to pay a hunting fine in Siler City.

199) Ramona Wiley's nickname for Barney was Squeaky.

200) Barney met Halcyon Loretta Winslow and her dad at Klein's Coffee House.

201) They "pull in the sidewalks" at 7 p.m. in Mayberry.

202) While in the army, Barney worked at the PX library on Staten Island.

203) Ellen, the lady manicurist, leaves Mayberry to get married.

204) Andy's fishing fine is $25.

194) False (Goober)

195) True

196) True

197) False (Siler City)

198) False

199) False (Tweeky)

200) True

201) False (9 p.m.)

202) True

203) True (to Pierre)

204) True

205) Briscoe doesn't spill food on his shirt.

206) Mrs. Lesch states that the Pilot Pines Funeral Parlor buried her husband.

207) Mrs. Lesch allegedly owes the funeral parlor $300.

208) According to Aunt Bee, as a young boy Andy lost 4 pounds after every bath.

209) Andy plays the bongos.

210) Melinda Keefer has fat knees and talks a lot.

211) Dud Wash's service in the Army totaled 5 years.

212) Andy said that Sam Becker might be planting lima beans or barley.

213) Barney said his #1 job is still-busting.

214) Goober once got out of a cave by following a skunk.

215) Opie and Johnny Paul sold seeds

216) Red Akin writes the column "Mayberry after Midnight."

217) Barney takes a picture of himself at the gas station.

205) False (He does spill on his shirt, he doesn't spill on his pants)

206) True

207) False ($140)

208) True (of dirt)

209) False (Barney does)

210) True

211) False (Three years)

212) True

213) False (stalking)

214) True

215) False (Andy and Barney did, as kids)

216) True

217) True

218) Charlotte Tucker's husband falls down a lot.

219) According to legend, Old Man Remshaw put his hired man in a straitjacket.

220) Barney recommends Andy put a Windsor knot in the old striped tie.

221) Barney, while posing as a criminal locked up with Doc Malloy, says that he has never been called "mad dog."

222) There are eleven stray dogs in the episode "Dogs, Dogs, Dogs."

223) Otis has a brother named Ned.

224) Mrs. Foster's "chicken a la king" tastes like wallpaper paste.

225) Andy hates white beans.

226) By Mayberry standards, "Bread, Love, and Beans" is a risqué movie.

227) Otis often drinks soda pop.

228) Aunt Bee tells Briscoe Darling that nice people don't spill at the table.

218) True

219) False (Put chains on him)

220) True

221) False (tattle-tale)

222) True

223) False (Otis' brother is named Ralph)

224) True

225) False (he ate four bowlfuls once)

226) True

227) False (He says it's bad for his liver)

228) True

229) Opie takes "nutrition money" to school on a regular basis.

230) Emma Brand makes a batch of pies every day.

231) Gomer runs his car over Barney's foot.

232) Andy refers to Freddie Fleet's band as "one of them traveling religions."

233) The Morrison Sisters start making wine after they quit making moonshine.

234) According to Barney, it's not a whim anymore if you change your shirt.

235) Goober's normal portion of pancakes is 12-15.

236) Gomer holds the Mayberry record for eating pancakes.

237) John Masters breaks out in hives when he gets upset.

238) Opie's favorite pie is cherry.

239) Opie gives an apple pie to Weary Willie the hobo.

240) Ernest T. Bass would tenderize a possum with licorice whips.

241) Juanita, the waitress at the diner, is never seen until the final episode.

229) True

230) True

231) False (Norbert runs over Barney's foot)

232) True

233) False (they put up preserves)

234) False (put on clean underwear)

235) True

236) False (Goober)

237) True

238) False (apple or butterscotch pecan)

239) True

240) False (Beats it with a stick)

241) False (never seen in any episode)

242) Otis drives his car into a river and drowns.

243) Mayberry has a gas station named "Cornwall's".

244) Barney weighs in at 148 ½ pounds.

245) Andy and Barney are cousins.

246) Barney hits Goober with a tomato.

247) Opie excels in arithmetic.

248) Barney gives Gomer a ticket for speeding.

249) Wally fires Gomer.

250) Barney once took Juanita to Morelli's.

251) Aunt Bee is kidnapped by Briscoe Darling

252) Aunt Bee is arrested for gambling

253) Warren is arrested for loitering

254) Helen goes skeet shooting with Andy

255) Opie wins a track and field medal.

256) Opie has a dog named Blackie.

257) Opie plays the guitar.

258) Barney has a cousin named Regis

242) False

243) True

244) False

245) True

246) False (he hit Otis)

247) False

248) False (making a U-turn)

249) True

250) True

251) True

252) True

253) False (gambling)

254) False

255) False

256) False

257) True

258) False

259) Andy saves Goober's life.

260) Goober once had a dog named Spot.

261) Lydia Croswaith has a bad back.

262) Floyd's Barber Shop was once a cover for a gambling operation.

263) Floyd is related to Otis.

264) Opie thought about joining the Navy.

265) Barney plays the piano.

266) Goober gets car sick.

267) Andy runs for mayor of Mayberry.

268) Ellie Walker runs for town council.

269) Newton Monroe sells Floyd a fur piece.

270) Malcolm Meriwether is English.

271) Andy dated Thelma Lou.

272) Andy is a widower.

273) Leon always wears a cowboy outfit.

274) Sarah, the operator, is only seen in one episode.

275) The Taylors house has a detached garage.

259) False (Gomer's)

260) True

261) True

262) True

263) False

264) True

265) False

266) False (Gomer)

267) False

268) True

269) False

270) True

271) False

272) True

273) True

274) False (she is never seen)

275) True

276) Aunt Bee had her own TV Show.

277) Barney was a member of his high school Spanish Club.

278) Barney moves from Mayberry to Mount Pilot.

279) Barney buys a car from old man Foley.

280) Howard is the county clerk.

281) Briscoe Darling plays the mandolin.

282) Walker's Drug Store serves ice cream.

283) Opie gives Helen a handkerchief as a gift.

284) Barney "wishes" for a finger print set.

285) Neil Bentley tells Floyd the suit he is wearing is made of snake skin.

286) Ellie Walker is a licensed pharmacist.

287) Otis sues the county of Mayberry.

288) Judy and Veronica are "The Fun Girls."

289) Barney sold vacuum cleaners.

290) Barney buys some "Miracle Salve."

291) Emmett buys his wife a fur coat.

292) Aunt Bee was a temporary deputy.

276) True (The Mayberry Chef)

277) True

278) False (Raleigh)

279) False

280) True

281) False (a jug)

282) True

283) False

284) True

285) False

286) True

287) True

288) False (Skippy and Daphne)

289) True

290) True

291) True

292) True

293) Andy plays the piano.

294) Bobby Fleet willfully auditions Jim Lindsey.

295) Thelma Lou is a waitress at the diner.

296) Barney holds a real estate license.

297) Barney receives a gold pen on his 5 year anniversary with the Sherriff's Department.

298) Emmett runs for City Council.

299) The Remshaw house has an axe on the basement door.

300) Opie buys his lunch at the school cafeteria.

301) Aunt Bee likes to fish.

302) Goober buys the service station from Wally.

303) Opie sets fire to a barn.

304) Gomer accidently locks himself in bank vault.

305) Otis once rode into town on a cow.

306) Barney receives 3 wishes from "The Count."

307) Goober once had a pet skunk

308) Barney becomes a detective in Raleigh.

309) Gomer arrests Barney.

293) True

294) False

295) False

296) True

297) False (a Watch)

298) True

299) True

300) False

301) False

302) True

303) False

304) False (Barney did)

305) True

306) False (1 wish)

307) True

308) True

309) True

310) Mr. Frisby's rooster is named Bo.

311) Howard writes a gardening column.

312) Andy has a boat named Annie.

313) Barney is on the Mayberry bowling team.

314) Barney always carries a loaded gun.

315) Andy is also a little league umpire.

316) Howard dates Flora from the diner.

317) Helen's niece gives Opie a black eye.

318) Barney can't wear a hat that has been on someone else's head.

319) Opie writes a paper about Andy as his most memorable character.

320) Howard once bowled a perfect game.

321) Red Skelton appeared on The Andy Griffith Show.

322) Howard buys a toaster from Newton Monroe.

323) The Mayor's office is directly above the courthouse.

324) Andy trades his favorite fishing pole for a sport coat.

325) Millie once dated Clyde Plot.

326) Opie calls sleeping outdoors adventure sleeping

310) True

311) True

312) False (Gertrude)

313) False

314) False (keeps one bullet in his shirt pocket)

315) True

316) False

317) True

318) True

319) True

320) True

321) False

322) False

323) True

324) False (bed jacket for Aunt Bee)

325) True

326) False (sleeping on an ironing board)

327) Barney's mother is never seen on the show.

328) Myer's Lake contains a silver carp nick named "Old Gus."

329) Opie once found a purse containing $50 in it.

330) Opie took piano lessons.

331) Barney lives with his mother.

332) Otis says his hobby is drinking.

333) There are 3 cells in the courthouse.

334) Barney took voice lessons.

335) Goober is a member of "The Regal Order of the Golden Door to Good Fellowship."

336) Andy plays the tuba.

337) The Sun is the name of Mayberry's newspaper.

338) Andy dislikes frozen dinners.

339) Asa is a security guard.

340) Barney sets a speed trap on Highway 6.

341) Barney had a bloodhound named "Spot."

342) Andy dated Peggy McMillan.

327) False

328) False

329) True

330) True

331) False

332) True

333) False (2)

334) True

335) True

336) True

337) False

338) False

339) True

340) True

341) False ("Blue')

342) True

343) Peggy's father is poor.

344) Helen Crump grew up in California.

345) Goober is the coach of the Mayberry Giants" baseball team.

346) Emmett sponsors the Mayberry bowling team.

347) Mayberry is located in South Carolina.

348) Mayberry is located in Pilot County.

349) Otis presents the town of Mayberry with a plaque.

350) It is said that Wally's has the best selection of soda pop in town.

351) Opie had a parakeet named Ricky.

352) Opie prints his own magazine.

353) Andy and Helen get married.

354) Barney tells Gomer about the gold shipment coming through town.

355) Floyd serves as a temporary deputy.

356) Barney once ran for sheriff of Mayberry.

357) Opie and Arnold convince a bank robber to confess.

358) Floyd has a son.

343) False

344) False (Kansas)

345) True

346) True

347) False (North Carolina)

348) False (Mayberry County)

349) True

350) True

351) False ("Dicky")

352) False

353) True

354) False (Laura Lee Hobbs told Gomer)

355) True

356) True

357) True

358) True

359) Howard has a daughter.

360) Howard lives with his mother.

361) Floyd is originally from Nashville.

362) Andy votes for Ellie for City Council.

363) Goober thinks Gilly Walker drives too fast.

364) Otis is a moonshiner.

365) Opie sells all of his Miracle Salve.

366) Barney pays "the little old lady from Mount Pilot" $300 for the car she is selling.

367) Opie destroys Aunt Bee's prized rose with a football.

368) Goober sends Barney a chain letter.

369) Opie's three wishes all come.

370) Ernest T. Bass wants to court Charlene Darling.

371) Andy carries a shovel and a rake in the squad car.

372) Charlene names her daughter after Opie.

373) Aunt Bee once wanted to marry Mr. Darling.

374) Barney thinks the book Robin Hood should be banned from the schools.

359) False

360) True

361) False

362) True

363) True

364) False

365) False

366) False ($297.50, the other $2.50 went to charity)

367) True

368) False (Floyd sent it to Barney)

369) True

370) True

371) True

372) False (after Andy)

373) False (Mr. Darling once wanted to marry Aunt Bee)

374) True

375) Andy throws a rock and breaks some glass.

376) Mayer Pike is chased up a tree by a bear.

377) Gomer tries to repair Aunt Bee's freezer.

378) Barney gets drunk on "mulberry squeezins."

379) Andy paid Jubal Foster to replace his barn.

380) Andy wins a percolator at the County Fair.

381) Clara Edwards has a son named Gale.

382) Andy sells the town cannon.

383) A haircut at Floyd's cost $1.00.

384) Otis spikes the water cooler in the courthouse.

385) Floyd wears contact lenses.

386) John Masters is the choir director.

387) Helen knows how to cook leg of lamb.

388) Andy usually carries a gun.

389) Barney usually wears a hat while on duty.

390) The squad car has two doors.

391) There are doilies on the cell chairs.

375) True

376) False (Mayor Stoner)

377) True

378) True

379) False

380) True

381) True

382) True

383) False ($1.75)

384) True

385) False

386) True

387) False

388) False

389) True

390) False (four)

391) True

392) Otis usually locks himself up on Saturday night.

393) Mr. McBeevee is Opie's imaginary friend.

394) Andy and Howard were once held hostage.

395) Wally's Gas Station has one gas pump.

396) Warren is a sleepwalker.

397) Aunt Bee is chosen to be the spokesperson for Foster's Furniture Polish.

398) Juanita is the town operator.

399) Charlene divorces Dud Wash.

400) Aunt Bee worked for counterfeiters.

401) Helen Crump's classroom has a portrait of Benjamin Franklin.

402) Floyd appeared on "Colonel Tim's Talent Time" TV show.

403) Gomer has a fear of spiders.

404) Helen has a niece named Cynthia.

405) Andy once arrested Aunt Bee.

406) Juanita works at the Junction Café.

407) Briscoe Darling has five boys.

392) True

393) False

394) True

395) False (two)

396) True

397) True

398) False (Sarah)

399) False

400) True

401) False

402) False (Howard)

403) True

404) True

405) True

406) True

407) False (four)

408) Barney nicknames his suit "Old Reliable".

409) Barney is allergic to horse hair.

410) The gun rack in the courthouse holds six guns.

411) Opie wins a basketball at the shooting gallery.

412) Gomer "takes off" on Cary Grant.

413) Goober joins the Marines.

414) The jail cell door keys are kept on a peg between the doors.

415) Barney organizes a women's softball team.

416) The courthouse contains three windows on the lower level.

417) Colonel Harvey sells his elixir for two dollars per bottle.

418) Malcolm Merriweather is an experienced falcon keeper.

419) Barney likes Mr. Cookie Bars.

420) Malcolm Tucker's car has a clogged fuel line.

421) A cat killed one of Opie's wild birds.

422) Howard has a speedboat.

423) Andy is read up on Grimms' Fairytales.

408) False (Salt and Pepper)

409) True

410) True

411) False

412) False (Goober)

413) False (Gomer)

414) True

415) False

416) True

417) False (one dollar)

418) True

419) True

420) True

421) False

422) False (Goober)

423) True

424) Howard once moved to the Caribbean.

425) Andy once ate three Mexican dinners in one night.

426) Barney and Otis were once held hostage by escaped convicts.

427) Goober gets a ticket for making a U-turn.

428) Weaver's Department Store sells "spirits."

429) Warren's last name is Newsome.

430) A parking fine in Mayberry is two dollars.

431) Andy once arrested Ben Weaver.

432) Wally's offers "Ethyl" brand gasoline.

433) Opie wins a pony.

434) Barney reads "True Blue Detective" magazine.

435) Gomer once lived with Andy.

436) Barney serves as Justice of the Peace in Mayberry.

437) Warren was a part-time deputy.

438) Barney and Andy square off in a public debate.

439) Goober dated Flora the waitress.

440) Howard and Millie travel together on a train.

424) True

425) False (Spaghetti)

426) False (Barney and Floyd)

427) False (Gomer and Barney)

428) True

429) False (Ferguson)

430) True

431) True

432) False (Acme)

433) False

434) True

435) True

436) False (Andy)

437) False

438) True

439) True

440) True

441) Barney once impersonated a pilot.

442) Clara Edwards plays the harp at church.

443) Floyd gave Andy his first haircut.

444) Aunt Bee once received the white bible in church.

445) Aunt Bee wears a blond wig to impress a man.

446) Gomer builds a car in the courthouse.

447) Barney hits a baseball through the window of the Remshaw house.

448) Aunt Bee and Clara Edwards write a hit song.

449) Floyd takes a second job selling insurance.

450) Barney once lived in the back room of the Courthouse.

451) Ernest T. Bass throws rocks with his left hand.

452) Howard once worked as a dance instructor.

453) Andy is superstitious.

454) Barney once got drunk with Otis.

455) Goober sings in the choir.

456) Fred Goss owns the "Mayberry Cleaners."

457) Leonard Blush wore a mask.

441) False

442) False (Organ)

443) True

444) False

445) True

446) False (Goober)

447) False (Opie)

448) True

449) False

450) True

451) False

452) False

453) False

454) True

455) False

456) True

457) True

458) Barney likes cashew fudge.

459) Mayberry does not have a phone book.

460) Mayberry's high school is named John Mayberry High.

461) Opie takes a job feeding a cow.

462) Andy and Gomer are relatives.

463) Barney often stays at the YMCA while on vacation.

464) One of Andy's favorite magazines is National Geographic.

465) Gomer goes on a date with Mary Grace Gossage.

466) Floyd punches Otis in the nose.

467) The courthouse is located on Elm Street.

468) Barney breaks a picture window with a slingshot.

469) Aunt Bee's last name is Parkins.

470) Bobby Fleet is a band leader.

471) Barney once posed as a mannequin.

472) The Andy Griffith Museum is located in Mt. Airy, North Carolina.

473) Mr. Ford is the president of the Mayberry Bank.

474) Leon always carries a bologna sandwich with him.

458) True

459) False

460) False (Mayberry Union High)

461) False

462) False

463) True

464) True

465) True

466) False

467) False (Main Street)

468) False

469) False (Taylor)

470) True

471) True

472) True

473) False (Mr. Meldrin)

474) False (Peanut Butter and Jelly)

475) There is a board game called Mayberry-Opoly.

476) There is a newspaper slot in one of the courthouse's front doors.

477) The Mayberry movie theater is named The Earle.

478) The Taylor's have one phone in their home.

479) Reverend Hobart Tucker is the preacher at the All Souls Church.

480) Goober once grew a beard.

481) Jim Lindsey is married.

482) Ellie Walker's is Fred Walker's daughter

483) Mrs. Medelbright married Oscar Fields.

484) The town newspaper is called The Mayberry Tribune.

485) The town newspaper is delivered on Wednesdays.

486) Jimmy is the name of the "loaded goat."

487) Joan was the name of the housekeeper before Aunt Bee.

488) Andy lives on Main Street.

489) Andy Taylor has a movie made about his life called "Truth, Justice and The American Way."

490) Mr. McBeevee gives Opie twenty-five cents.

475) True

476) False

477) False (The Grand)

478) False (Three)

479) True

480) True

481) False

482) False (niece)

483) False

484) False (Mayberry Gazette)

485) True

486) True

487) False

488) False (Maple Street)

489) False (Sheriff Without A Gun)

490) True

491) The Andy Griffith Show was filmed in North Carolina.

492) The best place for Andy Griffith Show merchandise is iMayberry.com.

493) There is a back door in the courthouse.

494) As of the writing of this book, the name of the actor who portrayed Mr. Schwamp is unknown.

495) The Andy Griffith Show has been on the air for over fifty years.

496) Goober punches Gilly Walker in the nose.

497) The Taylor's have a dog named Eddie.

498) Walker's Drug Store is located across the street from the courthouse.

499) Thelma Lou is a school teacher.

500) Andy plays the trombone.

491) False (California)

492) True

493) True

494) True

495) True

496) True

497) False

498) True

499) False

500) False

About The Author

Scott Hopkins was born and raised in the Midwest and is an avid fan of The Andy Griffith Show. He was involved extensively with the development of the Mayberry Mania Game and the Mayberry-Opoly game. Scott resides in Ohio with his wife, Tina, and daughters, Haley and Lily.

CPSIA information can be obtained
at www.ICGtesting.com
Printed in the USA
LVOW10s1604220817
545954LV00012B/885/P